# American Naturalism
# and the Jews

# American Naturalism and the Jews

## Garland, Norris, Dreiser, Wharton, and Cather

DONALD PIZER

UNIVERSITY OF ILLINOIS PRESS

Urbana and Chicago

Manufactured in the United States of America
C 5 4 3 2 1
∞ This book is printed on acid-free paper.

Library of Congress Cataloging-in-Publication Data
Pizer, Donald.
American naturalism and the Jews : Garland, Norris,
Dreiser, Wharton, and Cather / Donald Pizer.
p.  cm.
Includes bibliographical references and index.
ISBN 978-0-252-03343-8 (acid-free paper)
1. American literature—20th century—History and
criticism. 2. American literature—19th century—History
and criticism. 3. Jews in literature. 4. Antisemitism
in literature. 5. Naturalism in literature. 6. Authors,
American—20th century—Political and social views.
7. Authors, American—19th century—Political and
social views.
I. Title.
PS173.J4P59      2008
810.9'3529924073—dc22      2008006404

# Contents

# Acknowledgments

I would like to thank Stephen Brennan, Richard Lehan, Joseph R. McElrath, Keith Newlin, Thomas P. Riggio, and Fannie Yoker for their comments and aid in connection with various parts of this book in the course of its preparation. Also, a special kind of thanks to the late John Higham for his groundbreaking studies of late nineteenth- and early twentieth-century American anti-Semitism, *Strangers in the Land* and *Send These to Me*—special because Higham, as a young UCLA assistant professor of history, was on my doctoral examination committee these many years ago, and I recall his firm guidance and penetrating mind with pleasure.

I would also like to thank the Doheny Library, University of Southern California, and the Annenberg Rare Book and Manuscript Library, University of Pennsylvania, for permission to publish manuscript material from their Garland and Dreiser collections. Finally, thanks to *Dreiser Studies* for permission to publish (in revised form) "Dreiser and the Jews," which appeared in its Summer 2004 issue.

# Introduction

I have been writing for over fifty years about the generation of American writers who came to maturity in the 1890s and who are usually designated as naturalists. I have always been aware of the anti-Semitism present in the thinking of almost all of these writers, but since I believed that this was not a major element in their work, I put it aside. More recently, however, while editing Dreiser's interviews and then his letters, I came to realize that this strain had a more significant role in his career than I had previously understood. From my effort in a lengthy essay to explain and describe Dreiser's anti-Semitism I have moved on to an attempt in this volume to deal with the phenomenon in five of the major writers of the period.

What is intriguing in any consideration of the anti-Semitism of these writers is the contradiction between the regressive nature of this belief, with its underlying atavistic hate and fear of the stranger/outsider, and the more enlightened character of their values, writings, and activities in many other areas. These concerns range in nature and intensity from Dreiser's lifelong commitment to causes on behalf of the poor and oppressed, Garland's devotion to a wide range of social improvement activities for most of his career, Cather's and Wharton's espousal in their writing of feminist positions, and Norris's attack on corporate greed. Yet even though all these writers, especially Dreiser, Norris, and Garland, were in their own day frequently considered radical in their beliefs, they also expressed anti-Semitic ideas. Indeed, they often did so without any conscious awareness of a discrepancy between these viewpoints and their other values. In 1920, for example, Garland was asked to sign a letter protesting the rise of anti-Semitism in America. In the course of his reply refusing the request, Garland noted that he was a "reformer" who for forty years had been "an advocate for social betterment" in America. Nevertheless, he said elsewhere in the letter, it was necessary to "frankly admit the presence of an Internationalist Jew and to deplore the disturbing and embittering effect of his presence in America."[1] (The "Internationalist Jew," it should be explained, was Henry Ford's term, derived from his acceptance of the *Protocols of the Learned Elders of Zion* forgery, for Jews engaged in a conspiracy to control the finances and culture of all nations.)[2]

The question I seek to answer in this volume is that of how and why this contradiction occurred. The contradiction is, I believe, a distinctively American issue. Interpreters of nineteenth- and twentieth-century anti-Semitism as a worldwide phenomenon have often noted that anti-Semitism in America was principally rhetorical in nature while the European variety was activist.[3] Americans expressed anti-Semitic beliefs but, unlike European anti-Semites, they did not seek to translate these beliefs into riots or pogroms or oppressive law. It has not been noted, however, that, unlike the United States, most European anti-Semitism stemmed from writers and thinkers who were also conservative or reactionary in their other social beliefs. I wish to examine the sources and nature of anti-Semitism in this group of late nineteenth-century American writers to help explain how it was possible for them to find anti-Semitism palatable as a belief in the face of their strongly held liberal values concerning other areas of American social life.

The subtitle of this volume contains the names of the five authors I consider in the book in order to make clear that, despite the work's title, I do not intend the study to be inclusive for American literary naturalism as a whole. My interest rather is in a select group of writers born in the 1860s and '70s who came to maturity in the 1890s, who then constituted the major new force in American expression for several decades, and who expressed anti-Semitic beliefs.[4] The "naturalism" of these writers is not my focus; indeed, Garland and Cather are only seldom considered naturalists. But since all of the authors I discuss are of this generation and share in the naturalist desire to produce a more truthful American literature, I have adopted the term for the group as a whole. Of the significant writers of this generation whom I do not discuss, Stephen Crane, despite the large body of his work devoted to New York scenes, seldom alluded to Jews. Although Jews do play major roles in several of Harold Frederic's novels, this work occurs late in Frederic's career in English-set novels, after he had lived in England for many years, and is thus outside the American social currents I am interested in. Perhaps my most significant omission is Jack London, who, beginning around 1906, frequently expressed anti-Semitic ideas in his fiction and letters. But since London's anti-Semitism is never central to his writing, being largely in the form of brief authorial asides, and is also always both ideologically predictable and similar to Frank Norris's beliefs in this area, I thought that there would be little gained by his inclusion. Finally, Sherwood Anderson's and Charlotte Perkins Gilman's occasionally expressed anti-Semitism do not warrant full discussion, especially since Anderson's closely resembles Dreiser's and Gilman's echoes Wharton's and Cather's.

My intent, in other words, in selecting Garland, Norris, Dreiser, Wharton, and Cather for discussion is to have available for examination the careers and work of a diverse group of authors who flourished more or less contemporarily and who shared and expressed a similar prejudice. Some of the writers of this group were to the manor born (Norris and Wharton), some were of working-class or poor farmer background (Dreiser and Garland). Some were college bred (Norris, Cather), others were largely self-educated after high school or private tutoring (Dreiser, Garland, Wharton). Although all lived and worked for a time in New York, almost all were originally from various other parts of the country—Norris from the far West, and Garland, Dreiser, and Cather from the Midwest. And though all expressed anti-Semitic views, they did so in a variety of ways and at different moments of their careers, ranging from Garland's largely private comments in his letters and diaries to Norris's explicit anti-Semitic portraits in several of his major novels.

Despite their variations in backgrounds and careers and in the shape of their anti-Semitic expression, the five writers I discuss have in common a number of basic beliefs about Jews, beliefs derived principally from their shared experience of the social and ideological currents of their day. It should be clear from this statement that I will not be discussing the anti-Semitism of these writers from the standpoint of their personal psychological makeup. Of course, the distinctive temperament of each figure played some role in the matter—most obviously, perhaps, in the case of Dreiser, whose doubts about himself led him to be highly sensitive to what he believed were personal affronts by Jews. But in the matter of tracing the sources of an individual's anti-Semitism, I have largely heeded the counsel of Czeslaw Milosz, who himself emerged out of an intellectual and cultural climate stridently anti-Semitic at its core: that studies that stress the personal in examining the bases of anti-Semitism "rarely get to the heart of the matter because they overlook those peculiar traits that belong to geography and history rather than to psychology."[5] The anti-Semitism of the figures I discuss, in other words, is most productively discussed not as an aspect of a flawed personality but as a state of mind that took shape in response to various social, political, and literary movements of their day, all of which shared a disposition toward racist assumptions.

Historians of anti-Semitism in America have described a number of causes for the significant growth in the belief between the Civil War and World War II.[6] These include the persistence of the deicide charge, especially among the urban and rural poor; the strengthening of the Shylock image of the Jew as motivated principally by greed in a period when Jews were increasingly prominent in banking and merchandizing; the presence throughout the Midwest, stimulated by the Populist Revolt of the 1880s and '90s, of a conception of the Jew as a bloodsucking International Banker controlling the destiny of the area; the impact on American cities of the new Jewish immigration from eastern Europe after 1880; and the rise of racial theories antagonistic toward Jews throughout the late nineteenth and early twentieth centuries. Of these, the belief that Jews were culpable in the death of Christ does not appear to have played a role in the ideas of these writers. The Shylock image, however—the Jew as a symbol of greed—was pervasive, from Norris's and Dreiser's explicit use of Shylock figures to Wharton's and Cather's strong echo of the image. The belief that all Jews are Shylocks, however, is principally a symptom of other anti-Semitic currents in the culture. In the history of modern anti-Semitism, in other words, Shylock has always been present as a reservoir of anti-Semitic representation whose reappearance can be stimulated by events and ideas of the specific moment. In the brief introductory account that follows of the various currents of late nineteenth-century American anti-Semitism that influenced the writers I am examining, I therefore concentrate on the two major social events of the period that were most responsible for encouraging anti-Semitic belief: the western farmers' revolt and the East Coast patrician revulsion toward the new immigration; and on the two most important ideological positions buttressing the anti-Semitism encouraged by these events: beliefs about the degenerate or "Asiatic" character of the Jews as a race and complementary beliefs about the Anglo-Saxon origin of American culture. I will also be returning to all of these at various times in later chapters when it is necessary to explain more fully the relationship of these events and ideas to the beliefs of specific writers.

The Populist movement had its origin in the late 1880s during a prolonged agricultural depression that caught prairie-West farmers in the intractable dilemma of poor yields, low prices, and high mortgages.[7] Finding the major parties unresponsive to their problems, farmer organizations formed a third party, the People's (or Populist) Party, and contested state and national elections throughout the early 1890s. Radical in many of their principles—state control of railroads, banking, and land ownership were among their proposals—the Populists, as a grassroots movement led by stump orators, also demonized those they believed responsible for their economic woes by casting them in the role of rich eastern and foreign bankers, moneylenders, and bond holders who sought to suck them dry. Because many of these were, in fact, Jews—most infamously the international Rothschild banking firm—and because the image of the Jew as a Shylock exploiting the needs of those requiring financing was readily available in popular culture, it is not surprising that many Populist leaders adopted an anti-Semitic rhetoric. The Jew, within this rhetoric, was not a producer, as was the farmer, but a parasitical manipulator of money.[8] There were in fact few Jews in midwestern towns and villages of the 1880s and '90s against which to test these ideas, and in a sense any local testing was extraneous, for the Jew as Shylock in the midwestern imagination lived in splendor in an Eastern metropolis or London. As will become evident in the anti-Semitic ideas of Garland and Cather (both prairie bred) and, to a lesser extent, of Dreiser and Norris, the Populist notion of the Jew as a parasitic exploiter had an indelible effect on those raised in the midst of its open and emphatic expression.

A second major cause for the pervasiveness of anti-Semitic beliefs during the late nineteenth century was the great migration to America of largely impoverished East European Jews, who, stimulated by Polish and Russian pogroms, flocked to East Coast cities.[9] From the early 1880s to the early 1920s, when stringent new immigration laws came into effect, more than three million Jews immigrated, and in 1924 it was estimated that 44 percent of the population of New York was Jewish. This new immigrant stock, as has often been pointed out, did not resemble the relatively small and largely Germanic Jewish emigration of the antebellum period. The new settlers were poor and uneducated villagers, had few skills other than in the needle trades, and appeared uncouth and distinctly "foreign" in their way of life. They thus seemed to pose a threat to the long-present and largely Anglo-Saxon middle class of the areas in which they settled. Initially, this threat derived principally from the aura of the unsanitary and criminal adhering to the urban ghettoes in which their condition forced them to live. By the turn of the century, however, and reaching a high point in the first two decades of the new century, the challenge presented by urban Jews often consisted of their efforts to enter and to play major roles in the professions and in such commercial activities as marketing, entertainment, and publishing, and to translate their success in these and other areas into full acceptance in the mainstream of American life. The so-called patrician response to this threat—fully apparent in Garland's later career and in the ideas and work of Wharton and Cather—was to view with repugnance the effort of Jews to enter fully into American middle-class life.[10]

The poverty-stricken turn-of-the-century eastern European immigrant Jew was of course a striking instance of the "outsider" in a culture derived principally from northern Europe and now increasingly middle class. It was therefore not entirely an accident that several schools of racial theorizing arose during this period that served the purpose of legitimatizing on seemingly scientific grounds the folk fear of the outsider.[11] One such school, which originated in Europe and soon found American spokesmen, asserted that eastern European Jews were either of degenerate or Asiatic "blood," a racial heritage that accounted for their physical and temperamental differences from the Aryan peoples of northern Europe and that rendered them incapable of being assimilated into nations derived from that stock. "Oriental" was often a code term in this form of racial anti-Semitism, one that signified, as for example when used by Dreiser and Cather, an acceptance of the premise that it was impossible for Jews to be assimilated into American culture.

Less specifically anti-Semitic in origin, but still playing an important role in late nineteenth-century anti-Semitism with a racial basis, were the beliefs of the so-called Long March school of American historians, led by Herbert Baxter Adams of Johns Hopkins.[12] It was held by this group that American political institutions, as well as the American emphasis on the personal attributes of vigor and freedom, stemmed from the Anglo-Saxon tribes of northern Germany in that the primitive democratic values and practices of these groups were later transmitted by Anglo-Saxon migrations to England and then finally to the United States. No less a figure than Theodore Roosevelt strongly endorsed this view, and it was widely held throughout the last decades of the century. Here, unlike the notion of the Jew as unassimilable, the fear was that the Jew would indeed enter the largely Anglo-Saxon American racial pool and thus weaken and pollute it. Nevertheless, as will be seen for many of the writers I discuss, especially Norris, despite this apparent contradiction, the two racial theories—the Jew as degenerate or Asiatic and the "Long March" theory of history—complemented each within conventional anti-Semitic rhetoric. Put broadly and simply, as indeed many Americans conceived of the issue, the nation owed its greatness to its Anglo-Saxon heritage, and Jews, because they could not adapt to and live within the values and beliefs of this source, harmed or defiled it.

I do not wish to suggest by my citing of the relationship of a specific writer to a specific social event or ideology that it is possible to trace a single precise source for each writer's anti-Semitism. It is more useful, rather, as will be apparent from the chapters that follow, to conceive of the body of late nineteenth- and early twentieth-century anti-Semitic belief as a kind of pool from which a writer draws various ideas at different moments during his or her career, though often with a preference for one or two of these ideas.

American Naturalism
and the Jews

# 1

# Hamlin Garland

     The discussion of Garland's attitude toward the Jews that follows, I hasten to state at the beginning, is not an effort to paint him as an anti-Semite in any conventional sense of the term. Garland was not deeply preoccupied by the Jewish presence in American society for much of his career, and his comments about Jews lacked the rabid vehemence of the full-scale anti-Semite. Indeed, with the exception of his diaries and his last series of autobiographies (which themselves often derive from his diaries), his writings contain few direct references to Jews.[1] (As I will shortly seek to demonstrate, it is largely by his failure in two key contexts to discuss issues pertaining to Jews that he most reveals his beliefs.) Nevertheless, he shared with many Americans of the period various misgivings about the role of Jews in American life, and like most who were not convinced anti-Semites, he for the most part expressed these strains of concern either privately or obliquely. Garland's beliefs about the Jews are thus of considerable interest both because they reflect almost all the major threads in the makeup of late nineteenth- and early twentieth-century American anti-Semitism and because he neither shouted these beliefs from the rooftop nor actively sought to promote them as public policy. He appears to have been like many Americans of his day—responsive to negative interpretations of the "problem" presented by the American Jew but unwilling to pursue his concerns into overt expression or social activism. An exploration of the element of anti-Semitism in his career and expression is therefore of considerable interest because it suggests the widespread presence and nature of similar beneath-the-surface strains in the belief of his era.

I examine two phases of Garland's attitude toward the Jews: the first deriving from his participation in the farmers' revolt of the early 1890s and culminating in his Populist novel *A Spoil of Office* (1892); the second deriving from his residence in New York during the 1920s and culminating in his meetings with Henry Ford in the late 1920s.

Garland was converted to a faith in Henry George's single tax theory in late 1887, after returning to Boston from a trip home to the prairie west.[2] The poverty and hardship of Iowa and South Dakota farmers appeared to him to be both explainable and remediable in relation to George's assertion that the private ownership of land, often for speculative purposes, was the cause of the paradox of extreme poverty in a nation blessed with bountiful natural resources and an eager workforce. A second journey west, in the summer of 1888, in the midst of a deepening agricultural depression, confirmed him in this conviction, and for the next several years he gave much time and effort to furthering the single tax cause by frequently speaking on the subject, both in Boston and on western lecture tours, and by incorporating single tax themes into his western farm fiction.

During these years, from the late 1880s to early 1892, western farmers' organizations had become increasingly politicized. The loosely connected Grange associations of the post–Civil War decades were devoted principally to educational and social activities. By the late 1880s, the Farmers' Alliance began to supplement and then replace the Grange as a farmers' organization, but now one committed to speaking out on issues of importance to western farmers and to fielding political candidates in local and congressional elections under Alliance sponsorship, as it did with considerable success in 1890. During 1891 and 1892, leading up to the presidential election of 1892, the Farmers' Alliance reshaped itself, in a series of conventions, into a national political party, the People's Party (or Populists), with both presidential and congressional candidates.

Garland's own political sympathies and activities during 1887–92 mirrored what was occurring in the western farmers' revolt in general, a history that is indeed also reflected to a considerable degree in the career of Bradley Talcott, the autobiographical protagonist of *A Spoil of Office*. Initially, single taxers took a dim view of the Alliance and the Populists both because their traditional allegiance, following the lead of George himself, was with the Democratic party, and because of a realization that farmers looked askance at any reform that threatened, as did single tax beliefs, private ownership of land. But Garland found during his several research, lecturing, and campaigning trips to the West during the early 1890s that the two reform-minded groups were compatible. Many Populist proposals—especially those involving government regulation of railroads and banks—were also supported by single taxers, and a considerable number of Alliance and then People's Party leaders were amenable to land ownership reform. Indeed, the famous Omaha Platform of July 1892, which set out the Populist program for the forthcoming election, contained what was widely regarded as a single tax plank.[3]

It is not surprising, therefore, that Garland's own activities shifted during these pivotal years of 1887–92 from that of fervent spokesman for the single tax to that of an equally intense supporter of a People's Party with a single tax slant. He clearly revealed this evolution in a lecture to the Chicago Single Tax Club in January 1892:

> I was prejudiced against the Alliance . . . before I went out to study it. Not that I questioned the honesty of its motives, or the general intelligence and patriotism of its adherents. But I regarded its methods as doubtful, and its aims as foolish, if not worse. When I got among the farmers, however, and really got an understanding of their position, I changed my mind. I found they were not so far wrong after all. They are not pig-headed and reactionary. On the contrary, they are alive to new ideas and willing to be set right if it can be shown they are wrong. They eagerly heard me in advocacy of the single tax. . . . So I have cut loose from the old moorings and have thrown myself heart and soul into the farmers' movement.[4]

Garland's reference to have "got among the farmers" refers to two extended trips to the West during this period. During the winter of 1890–91, in response to a suggestion from B. O. Flower of the *Arena* that Garland write a novel about the farmer's revolt, he spent several months in the West lecturing to single tax groups and conducting research. In the fall of 1891, he journeyed to Iowa and Kansas to observe and participate in the off-year local elections occurring in those states.[5]

Populism has received a great deal of attention from historians both because it was a major force in American politics during the 1890s, with its supporters electing numerous congressmen and senators and largely responsible for the rise of William Jennings Bryan to national prominence, and because many of its reform proposals were indeed gradually adopted. Initially, historians interpreted Populism largely in relation to its radical belief that it was necessary to curb the power of huge trusts and corporations in order to return the country to its Jeffersonian roots of freedom of opportunity for all. In the mid-1950s, however, Richard Hofstadter challenged this view by describing at length the strain of paranoid nativism present in Populist thought and expression, an element that included a distinct and oft-repeated anti-Semitism. For proof of this claim Hofstadter concentrated on the published writings of three of the most prominent figures in the movement: Ignatius Donnelly, William H. Harvey, and Mary Elizabeth Lease.[6]

Donnelly, a Minnesotan who played a major role in creating the People's Party and who wrote the preamble to its 1892 party platform, published in 1890 the anti-utopian novel *Caesar's Column.* The central conceit of the novel is that most of the world by the late twentieth century is controlled by Jewish financiers. In America, the representative of this group is Prince Cabano (born Jacob Isaacs), who through his great wealth and a cabal of rich fellow Jews controls every aspect of American life. (He also keeps a harem of beautiful young Gentile women.) The plot of the novel centers on the efforts of the Brotherhood, a revolutionary organization whose political ideals resemble those of the Farmers' Alliance and the Populists, to overthrow Cabano.

William H. Harvey was commonly known as "Coin" Harvey because of the immense popularity of his 1894 study *Coin's Financial School,* which sold a million copies during its first year in print. Written in response to the tendency within Populism after 1892 to center more and more on the gold issue, Harvey's exercise in popularized economics squarely places the blame for the farmer's woes on the domination of the money market by foreign banks, especially British, which rely on the scarcity of gold to keep money in short supply and therefore mortgage rates high. Harvey, who also published in 1894 the anti-Semitic novel *A Tale of Two Nations,* which dramatizes the demonetization of silver as a Jewish conspiracy, made clear the anti-Semitic thrust of his charge by a famous cartoon that appears in *Coin's Financial School.* A huge octopus, labeled Rothschild, sits in London on a pot of gold while its enveloping tentacles squeeze the life out of the rest of the world.[7]

The anti-Semitic coding of Populist rhetoric in the work of Donnelly, Harvey, and other leaders in the movement is obvious, as indeed was necessary if it was to be widely understood. Put simply, there was a conspiracy by foreign banks—the "international gold ring"—to milk farmers dry, with British banks and Jewish bankers, and especially the Rothschilds, in the forefront of this effort. The rhetoric had great appeal, as later commentators have pointed out, not only because it relied on the inherent paranoia of any oppressed group but because it also drew upon threads of the Shylock and deicide beliefs present in rural populations. The peroration of William Jennings Bryan's 1896 speech accepting the presidential nomination owes its amazing resonance in its own time to its echoing of these rhetorical threads:

"You shall not press down upon the brow of labor this crown of thorns. You shall not crucify mankind upon a cross of gold."[8]

Hofstadter's charges did not go unanswered, and for several decades there was a lively debate among academic historians as to whether he was guilty of exaggerating the importance of a few Populist leaders or whether he had indeed only uncovered the tip of the iceberg of western agrarian anti-Semitism. Today there exists an uneasy truce—not so much a consensus as an acceptance that there were anti-Semitic elements in Populist rhetoric but that it is possible to overemphasize their importance in both Populist belief and policy.

Mary Elizabeth Lease's participation in Populist anti-Semitism is of great interest in relation to Garland's involvement in the movement because there is considerable evidence that she served as the principal model for his portrait of Ida Wilbur, the heroine of *A Spoil of Office*.[9] Garland recalled that he wrote his novel of the farmers' revolt in late 1891 by cobbling together a discarded manuscript dealing with an Iowa youth and observations derived from his own recent travel and research. In the novel, Bradley Talcott, a young Iowa lawyer who is also an effective orator, is elected as a Democrat first to the Iowa legislature and then to Congress. He has met early in his career the attractive Grange speaker Ida Wilbur, and he continues to encounter her in Des Moines and Washington. In the course of the novel, she gradually discards her Grange-inspired nonpolitical stance for a full endorsement of Farmers' Alliance and then Populist beliefs and activism, and by its close has both persuaded Bradley in the rightness of her new convictions and has accepted his proposal of marriage. Published serially in the *Arena* in the January through June 1892 issues, the novel clearly reveals its overproximity to Garland's recent experiences and intense convictions. He himself, much later in his career, echoed almost all critics of the novel when he wrote that "my grandiose plan for a panoramic novel of agricultural unrest degenerated into a partisan plea for a stertorous People's Party" in which his hero and heroine, the principal exemplars of this plea, "failed to hold the interest of my readers."[10]

Born in 1853, Mary Elizabeth Lease moved as a young woman with her family to a Kansas claim. By the late 1880s she was married with four children but had also earned a law degree and had embarked on a career as a Grange speaker. She came into national prominence in the elections of 1890, when her fiery stump oratory helped Farmers' Alliance state and congressional candidates capture Kansas. By most contemporary accounts she was not physically attractive—an impression confirmed by surviving photographs[11]—but she was blessed, in a period before amplification, with a much commented upon powerful contralto voice that held and moved her audiences. She continued to campaign vigorously on behalf of Populist causes and candidates in the elections of 1891 and 1892, but her rejection of the Populist drift toward a national alliance with the Democrats—a move sealed by the Populist endorsement of Bryan in 1896—led to the dimming of her role in the farmers' movement and of her fame.

In his *A Son of the Middle Border* account of his participation in the farmers' revolt, Garland briefly mentions Lease, "with Cassandra voice," as a Populist leader.[12] It is certain he had met her by the summer of 1892, when he and she shared a platform as speakers at a single tax rally held during the Populist presidential convention.[13] But it is also highly probable that they met during the fall 1891 campaign to elect Populist state and local candidates in the Iowa and Kansas elections. In *A Son of the Middle Border,* Garland recalled his participation "in meetings of rebellious farmers in bare-walled Kansas school-houses" and his encountering at this time, when Lease was also campaigning heavily in Iowa and Kansas, "many of the best known leaders in the field."[14] In one authoritative account, she and Garland are described as sharing a Des Moines platform on election night in early November 1891.[15] Although Garland was to transform Lease in *A Spoil of Office* in a number of ways to make her a suitable romantic heroine—Ida Wilbur is younger, attractive, and unmarried—he preserved in his portrait the basic lineaments of her career and beliefs. Like Lease, Ida is prairie raised, has had a speaking career in the Grange and Farmers' Alliance, and has grown into a conviction that a national political party—the People's Party—is necessary if the farmers are to achieve their goals. Perhaps most important, Lease and Ida share Garland's own distinctive reform enthusiasms within the more general Populist proposals for banking and railroad reform—an emphasis on woman's rights, above all suffrage, and the need for land reform along single tax lines.

What is absent entirely in Garland's portrait of Ida Wilbur as a Populist orator modeled on Lease is Lease's pronounced reliance on the anti-Semitic strain in Populist belief and rhetoric. Hofstadter was among the first to pick up on this element in her thinking and speeches, and it has since been further commented upon by others. Walter Nugent, in 1963, summed up Lease's beliefs as those of a "fervid exponent of Anglo-Saxon superiority, a racist," and noted that she was "responsible for far more of her share of references to Shylock, Rothschild, Jewish bankers, and British gold."[16] A passage from an 1896 speech captures the substance and tone of her rhetoric in this area: "The aristocracy of gold . . . despises governments, it tramples upon the rights of individuals, it scoffs at justice, it sneers at everyone, makes the golden rule subservient to the golden calf, and has made the Christian nations of the earth collecting agents for the house of Rothschilds. . . ."[17] Aside from fragments of Lease's speeches reported by newspapers, the major published record of her beliefs is her pamphlet *The Problem of Civilization Solved* (1895). The work contains a chapter entitled "Finance" that is shot through with explicit anti-Semitic statements and attributes all the ills of the western farmer to the monetary actions of international Jewish bankers. Grover Cleveland, the sitting president, she also later comments, is "an agent of Jewish bankers and British gold."[18]

It is difficult to accept that Garland was not aware of this strain in Lease's belief. There is little to suggest in Lease's career and recorded expression that she was reluctant to express her views in this area frequently and explicitly, because she was essentially, as is Ida, a stump orator who was appealing to an audience for whom the rhetoric of a foreign, non-Christian group of con-spirators controlling their fate satisfied the human need for a readily identi-fiable enemy. There are several possible explanations for this omission. It is plausible that Garland, in transforming Lease into Ida, erased this element in her thinking (and indeed in Populist rhetoric in general) in order to pre-serve her role as a representation of the high idealism of the Populist cause. For many in a national readership, an open expression of anti-Semitism by a Populist heroine would have been a confirmation of rural bigotry. But there is also the possibility that Garland, although he might have found Lease's racial beliefs embarrassing in their folk openness and intensity, was also not entirely unsympathetic to their basic cast and therefore found nothing incompatible between Lease's beliefs in this area and Ida's role as a Populist heroine. In the essay "Literary Masters" in his *Crumbling Idols* (1894), Gar-land wrote that it was his

> sincere conviction, taking the largest view, that the interior is to be hence-forth the real America. From these interior spaces of the South and West the most vivid and fearless and original utterance of the coming American democracy will come.
>
> This is my conviction. I might address arguments based on the differences in races; I might speculate upon the influence of the Irish and Jews and Ital-ians upon New York and Boston, and point out the quicker assimilation of the Teutonic races in the West. . . .[19]

Of course, the racism of this passage is one in which the Jews are lumped with other more recent and less desirable racial stock in the East and in which the stress is on their pollution of the literary expression of an older western Anglo-Saxon stock. There is nothing here about the control of the economic well-being of a section of the nation by foreign Jews. But the cast of mind that expressed the literary bias is clearly one that could accept the economic canard. In both instances, the West is threatened by a racial strain inimical to its well-being. Garland's omission in his portrait of Ida Wilbur of any reference to Lease's anti-Semitism may thus be in part a reluctance to complicate his depiction of a noble idealism fighting for an ideal cause. But in finding Lease's racial bigotry no hindrance to drawing upon her for this role, and in indeed making no reference at any time to this strain in Populism as a whole, Garland has, it would seem, indirectly revealed his own bias in this area.

The second phase of Garland's reflection of contemporary anti-Semitic beliefs has its origin in his move in 1884 from the Middle West to Boston in order to undertake a career in the Eastern intellectual and cultural center of American life. His gradual absorption over the next several decades of an Eastern patrician distaste for the presumed vulgarity and materialism of the immigrant hordes crowding into America's great cities was encouraged both by the racist historiography of the period and by his residence in New York City from 1916 to 1930. It received sporadic expression in his private diary and published autobiographies, but is most usefully revealed in his adulation of Henry Ford in the late 1920s.

Jews were not a large-scale presence in the middle-border West of Garland's youth, as is suggested by their complete absence from his stories and novels set on the farms and small towns of 1870s and 1880s Wisconsin, Iowa, and South Dakota. (It was only in 1895, in *Rose of Dutcher's Coolly*, when Rose comes to Chicago to live, that a Jew appears in his fiction, and then only briefly.) But by the time Garland came east in 1884, however, the great migration of eastern Europeans Jews to America was in full swing, with Garland experiencing it at firsthand, initially in Boston and then, and most fully, in New York. It is uncertain whether he also encountered during this period the increasingly strident nativist reaction to the presence of millions of East European Jews in America's great East Coast cities. Although Garland never alluded to specific writers or books espousing belief in the racial inferiority of the Jews, he nevertheless echoed ideas similar to their views throughout his later career whenever he took up the recent ethnic transformation of America. Indeed, one can find such an echo as early as 1894, in the passage from *Crumbling Idols* cited earlier, when he stated that the more prevalent "Teutonic" element in the western states made the area a better vehicle for the expression of American democratic belief than New York, which suffered under the impact of recent immigration by Irish, Italians, and Jews. It is, however, when he actually lived in New York, sporadically during the 1890s and the first decade of the new century and then consecutively for fifteen years beginning in 1916, that his views in this area both hardened and grew more frequent.

Garland's observations about Jews in his diaries and autobiographies have several general characteristics. For one, they reveal that although he appeared to have no close Jewish friends, he did admire a number of Jewish acquaintances who were either in the arts, such as the British writer Israel Zangwill and the American poet Arthur Guiterman, or who derived from long-settled Germanic stock and had made vast fortunes in America, such as the Guggenheim brothers, Otto Kahn, and the Lewisohn sisters.[20] In addition, he is more frank in writing about Jews in his diary than in his published reminiscences in the sense that negative remarks about Jews in the published work often group Jews with other recent immigrant stock rather than isolate them for special attention, as is common in the diaries. And finally, his negative comments about Jews increase in scope and vehemence over the years from initial concern and distaste because of their alien appearance, habits, and preoccupations to fears about their adverse impact on the cultural fabric of the nation to approval of attempts to control that impact.

After attending the theater in New York in late 1906, Garland recorded in his diary that "[t]he city crowds seemed very alien, very European and very wild to me. A mad throng filled Broadway, and the faces in the cars were all foreign—few familiar types" (29). Garland's vague sense of unease during this period—the unease of the "native" in the face of the "foreign"—could also take a more sharply focused form in regard to Jews in particular. While lecturing in Pittsburgh in February 1910, he meets a young Jewish journalist and comments, "He is young, able, and sees both sides of the problem. He is American but not as I am an American. Much depends on men like this young Jew. His leadership is vital. Can they assimilate? *Or* will they assimilate us?" (251). The two comments define the Jewish "problem" in Garland's mind at this stage. Jews are foreign—not American as I am—whatever their degree of assimilation, and he also fears that their inability to assimilate will alter the society in which they function and will thus alter the meaning of what it means to be an "American."

Once permanently settled in New York after 1916, Garland's beliefs that Jews constitute a distinctive and undesirable element in American culture and that it is uncertain whether they are capable of assimilation increase in frequency and intensity of expression. Returning in August 1917 from his Catskill summer home (in a restricted community, by the way), he finds himself on the train with

> the most amazing collection of New York Hebrews. Pink, brown, hook-nosed, straight-nosed, young, old—all chattering or brawling. They mobbed the train. They shoved, elbowed, pulled and pushed for seats, clamoring, shouting, all in perfect good humor. They were not poor, nor illiterate, but they were without a particle of reserve or politeness. Their nasal voices silenced all other outcry. The few "Americans" on the train were lost in this flood of alien faces, forms, and voices. . . . From a humanitarian point of view I should have been glad of their number for they were returning from a happy outing but as I was lame, their jostling greediness made me angry and their lack of the ordinary civilities of life disgusted me. (252)

The following year, after lecturing at a New York high school where almost all the students and teachers were Jewish, Garland pursued the theme inherent in his Catskill journey of a weakened native overwhelmed by an alien culture into the specific problem offered by the effort to transform that culture into one more "American" in nature. He noted in his diary (as later recorded in *My Friendly Contemporaries*): "So long as our teachers are carrying on the traditions of the republic, there is a possibility that the pupils can be made over into Americans, but when instructors as well as pupils become alien, there is danger that the principles and policies which hold our great nation together may be weakened."[21] Indeed, writing in *Back-Trailers from the Middle Border* a year later about Jewish domination of New York cultural life, he made explicit the baleful consequences for traditional American literary expression of this failure to "convert" an alien race. Jews, he noted, tended to congregate in cities, and "these concentration camps of foreign-born residents, many of them not citizens, had begun to affect our art, our drama, our fiction—in some ways to the good, but more often to the bad. The moving picture, the sensational press, and the brutal novel flourished in this rank soil. In the reek of the city an anti-American, anti-Puritan criticism had developed. . . ."[22]

During the early 1920s, when Congress, having fully accepted the position that the country had attracted too many "alien" cultures, passed a series of highly restrictive immigration laws, Garland on several occasions indicated his support of additional measures to combat or limit the impact of Jews on American intellectual life. In *Afternoon Neighbors* he noted his approval in late 1922 of Stuart Sherman's *Americans,* a book that restated Sherman's New

Humanist defense of traditional values. "Some of his comment," Garland wrote, "is especially needed now when so many Poles, Russians, Germans, Jews, and lately arrived critics are assuming to speak for all America. Sherman's book presents the English-American traditions . . ." (10). And in one of his most specific endorsements of the Anglo-Saxon theory of American development, he wrote in his January 1923 diary in relation to the much-publicized effort by President Abbott Lowell to restrict Jewish admission to Harvard that

> [h]ere again is an indication of the rising tide of Americanism. The Jew is in most cases alien to our traditions in fact as well as in appearance. Unless we rigidly exclude Jewish immigration the hatred of them will increase. It is quite within the bounds of possibility that violent measures will be taken to keep them in what the other races regard as their place. Rightly or wrongly this antagonism will grow. After all this nation is Anglo-Saxon. Not even two million German, Polish, and Russian Jews can alter that fact. But with millions in Poland, Russia, and Germany eager to come to us, New York is in danger of being swamped with them. Already we are "Jew York" to the Midwest. (253)

By 1926, as is suggested by a March diary entry of that year, Garland's concern over the overwhelming Jewish presence in the life of New York had taken on the tone of paranoiac overstatement: "The Jews," he wrote, "are gaining possession of courts, the law business, publishing, theater, moving pictures and by the weight of their numbers and wealth they will soon control the expression of opinion here. And as the whole nation gets a large part of its information from here, that information is un-American at its very source" (255).

It was during this period of the late 1920s, when Garland's long-present antagonism toward the Jewish presence in America was at its most strident, that he engaged in a significant relationship with Henry Ford, then the most famous and outspoken anti-Semite in the country.[23] Garland visited Ford, whom he had never met before, on several occasions during this period: in mid-December 1926, when he and his daughter Constance were in Detroit to give their lecture and reading performance on middle border pioneering and were invited by Ford to visit him in nearby Dearborn; in April and May 1927, when he met with the *Dearborn Independent* staff at Dearborn to discuss possible contributions to the newspaper and also spoke with Ford at his Dearborn home and at the Dearborn Country Club; and in June 1928, when Garland and his wife visited the Fords at their Dearborn estate.

Ford at this time was one of the most well-known men in the world. His au-

tomobile manufacturing and sales empire dominated the field, and he still ran it with an iron hand. He and Thomas Edison were almost universally admired as farm boys who through inventive genius and brilliant entrepreneurship had risen to full expression of the American dream. His various enthusiasms were therefore widely reported, as were his frequent utterances on political or social matters. Since 1920, however, Ford was also firmly associated in the public awareness with a virulent and blatant form of anti-Semitism. He had purchased in 1919 the *Dearborn Independent,* a weekly newspaper whose principal function was to serve as an outlet for his ideas. From May 1920, the journal engaged in what one historian has called "the greatest barrage of anti-Semitism in American history."[24] For almost two years, each issue contained at least one anti-Semitic article, many of them based on the *Protocols of the Learned Elders of Zion,* an infamous late nineteenth-century forgery that detailed the supposed plot by international Jewry to control the world through financial trickery. The articles also often dealt with the insidious Jewish infiltration of almost every phase of American life, especially the entertainment industry. The *Independent* had the extraordinary circulation, for a small-town newspaper, of between a quarter and a half million during this period. In addition, its anti-Semitic diatribes were almost immediately collected in a series of volumes under the collective title *The International Jew,* which also sold widely both in America and, in translation, abroad.

Ford's anti-Semitism bred a reaction in the form of a boycott of Ford cars, and Ford was led to suspend the *Independent*'s campaign in January 1922. It was renewed again, however, on a more modest scale, in November 1922, and continued until early 1925, when it largely ceased in response to a libel suit against Ford and the journal. The suit came to trial in the spring of 1927, and was major news for several months. When it appeared that the case was going badly for the *Independent,* Ford settled out of court. The issue of Ford's anti-Semitism then became less headline news until 1933, when it was revived by Ford's acceptance from Adolph Hitler of Germany's highest public honor. (*The International Jew* had served as a text for Nazi ideology since the early 1920s.)

Garland's writing about his visits to Ford during this highly volatile phase of Ford's public image took two forms. (His few pieces in the *Independent* itself consist of recycled older material and are of no interest.) He drafted an article in late 1926 based on his first visit, but failing to find a magazine willing to publish the piece, he put it aside.[25] (It is preserved in the Garland Collection at the University of Southern California.) And in the last volume of his autobiographical series dealing with his literary career, *Afternoon Neighbors*

(1934), he included lengthy sections dealing with each of his three encounters with Ford. Because Garland's unpublished essay "The Homely Side of Henry Ford" is relatively short, and because it contains nothing that was not later incorporated into the more detailed and full accounts of all three visits in *Afternoon Neighbors* (pp. 359–68, 398–405, and 503–11), I depend in my discussion of Garland and Ford on his published version.

The Ford projected by Garland in his accounts of their three meetings is almost entirely that of a lover of children, of the old ways of American life, and of a simple home existence. All three of these characteristics are present, for example, in the several extended passages in which Garland describes Ford's efforts to instruct children in pioneer American dances and musical instruments. Garland alerts the reader to Ford's reputation as "the mighty manufacturer, the monopolist, the ruthless standardizer, the despot" (360), but his principal effort is to convince the reader that "[t]here was something so gentle, so kindly and so fine in Ford's action and speech that I could not relate him to the bogey man which newspapers had built up" (361). He and Ford talk repeatedly of "the old time America" (362), and Garland is also introduced to Ford's enthusiasm for preserving the artifacts of America's pioneer past. His American farm equipment museum, Garland realizes, "has much in common with what I am doing in my Middle Border books" (367).[26] He remarks to Ford that "[t]hese utensils and furnishings tell of those who toiled—your forbears and mine" (364). At only one point does Garland even remotely refer to the universal awareness of Ford's campaign against the Jews, when his comments on Ford's remarks to him during a dinner at the Dearborn Country Club appear to allude to the frequent claim in the *Dearborn Independent* that Jews controlled international banking: "He uttered some extreme judgments, the kind of pronouncements which have laid him open to criticism, but for the most part his comment was kindly, shrewd and without assertion. He is an internationalist in theory but does not commend the bankers who practice it to their personal advantage" (401).

On the whole, Garland appears in these accounts to be seeking to whitewash Ford of his anti-Semitism, by refusing to acknowledge its existence, as thoroughly as he had done in re-creating Mary Elizabeth Lease as Ida Wilbur some thirty-five years earlier. In both instances, his motive was roughly the same. Both Lease and Ford represented older American beliefs that Garland himself deeply valued—Lease's of a Jeffersonian idealism in Populist form, Ford's of a deep-seated nostalgia for a simpler American past. For both Lease and Ford, anti-Semitic ideology stressing the Jew as a nonproductive manipulator of international finance had played a significant role in their beliefs and rhetoric. Indeed, John Higham, a major historian of American anti-Semitism, finds Ford's beliefs about a world Jewish banking conspiracy squarely in the late nineteenth-century agrarian political tradition.[27] It is not surprising, therefore, that Garland—given the powerful resonance that Lease's and Ford's beliefs had in his own mind, and given as well his misgivings about many aspects of the Jewish presence in American culture—was able to participate in the anti-Semitism associated with these figures to the extent of ignoring it in his idealized dramatizations of their strengths.

These two incidents toward the beginning and end of Garland's long career suggest that he was always handicapped in his response to experience by a kind of village mentality. What was strange and unfamiliar to him was threatening unless it was so exotic (as with the Indians) as to be merely exotic. He had a deep vein of sympathy for the oppressed, but he also preferred for almost all his life the familiar and his own kind of people. Circumstances gradually caused the unfamiliar and threatening to take the form of the urban Jew, but that frame of mind was present from the start and was therefore capable of finding nothing untoward in eliminating an element in Populist belief and Lease's rhetoric that may have been a blemish to others but which rang a harmonious chord in his own deepest nature.

I began this chapter, however, with the claim that Garland was not an anti-Semite in any conventional sense of the term. He did not engage in anti-Semitic activities, he did not portray Jews negatively in his fiction, and his writing about the shortcomings of Jews in his diaries and autobiographies is never virulent. But he nevertheless shared with many of his time a belief that the Jews represented a problem at best and a danger at worst to American society. One way in which he expressed this concern—by not acknowledging the presence of a virulent anti-Semitism in figures such as Lease and Ford—is probably compatible as well with the common middle-class American tendency to express a nonactivist anti-Semitism in as seemingly discreet and inoffensive a manner as possible.

# 2

# Frank Norris

Frank Norris's racism, which includes one of the most vicious anti-Semitic portrayals in any major work of American literature, has long been an embarrassment to admirers of the vigor and intensity of his best fiction and has also contributed to the decline of his reputation during the past several generations. It would be easy in Norris's case, given the range and consistency of his racial biases, to attribute this aspect of his beliefs to a personal flaw. But although there may indeed be a psychological misalignment in Norris's deepest nature that contributed to his bigotry, it is both more feasible and productive to examine the sources and nature of his anti-Semitism in relation to his distinctive historical moment.

The salient biographical facts bearing on the sources of Norris's beliefs are that he was brought to California by his parents in his early teens and that he attended the University of California from 1890 to 1894. He was therefore not only Californian in the usual sense of someone responsive to far western regional concerns but also in that he was exposed at Berkeley to ideas that deeply affected and colored his interpretation of these concerns. Readers of Norris are apt to forget, given the frequent and explicit anti-intellectualism of his literary essays, that, unlike most of the major writers of his period, he went to college for four years and that he encountered among several of his most vibrant teachers at Berkeley a shared contemporary view of the history of human development that tended to reinforce local biases. In order to make clear the connection between the racist threads in Norris's fiction and the beliefs of his time and place, I first discuss one of his important stories, "A Case for Lombroso" (1897), and then trace back its racist ideas to those he encountered and absorbed during his California years. I then examine the most blatant and troublesome manifestation of these ideas, his anti-Semitism, in *Vandover and the Brute, McTeague,* and *The Octopus.*

"A Case for Lombroso," which appeared in the San Francisco *Wave* in September 1897, is one of a series of stories that Norris wrote for the *Wave* about the mores of the San Francisco younger set of which he was a member.[1] Stayne is a San Francisco "thoroughbred." California bred and Harvard educated, he has matured into a handsome young man who is well-liked by all "because of his genuineness and his fine male strength and honesty and courage" (127). Put into the racial terms that were central to Norris's beliefs, he represents the Anglo-Saxon strain in America's racial past. His forefathers had fought their way from northern Europe to England and then to and across America by dint of strength of will and arms, and in doing so had cultivated as well a passion for individual freedom. On the other hand, because Cresencia is of California Spanish descent, her "race was almost exhausted, its vitality low" (128), a deficiency that makes her oversensitive, willfully self-centered, and emotionally unstable. "The red-hot, degenerate Spanish blood of her sang in her veins" (129). She is, Norris repeats several times, a "young girl of degenerate blood and jangled nerves and untamed passions" (130).

In a kind of allegory of the dangers of racial mixing, and, more specifically, of the danger of mixing the robust Anglo-Saxon strain with the degenerate Mediterranean, Stayne and Cresencia destroy each other. He initially cultivates her as a possible conquest, but when he realizes that she wishes to claim him permanently and attempts to end the relationship, she unleashes her anger and passion and draws him back despite his mistreatment of her. At the close of the story, they are locked in a sadomasochistic prison of pain. She takes "a strange, perverted pleasure in . . . submitting to his brutalities" (131), and it becomes "a morbid, unnatural, evil pleasure for him to hurt and humiliate her" (132).

"A Case for Lombroso" is irretrievably marred as a short story by Norris's formulaic rendering of a simplistic racial ideology, but it is this very quality that also provides a gateway to his beliefs in this area. The story is permeated with themes and language associated with racial fear. The most dynamic and fruitful racial strain in America's past, the Anglo-Saxon,[2] is threatened by a degenerate southern European element, and sex is the means by which that degeneracy both expresses itself and brings its victim down to its own level. The place of publication for "A Case for Lombroso," the San Francisco *Wave,* is significant in this regard. Norris was a staff member of the magazine between early 1896 and early 1898 and contributed to nearly every weekly issue during that time. Initially founded to appeal to "Those in the Swim" in the Bay Area,[3] it continued throughout its existence to stress California material and topics. One such area of great importance to Californians during this period was the threat presented to their outpost of "American" civilization by such presumed inferior races as the Chinese and Mexicans. For most of California's half-century as an American state, members of these two races had served as a source of cheap labor, the Chinese initially for railroad construction and Mexicans for work on ranches and farms.[4] As Norris suggests in a brief comment by Marcus Schouler in *McTeague*,[5] the questions both of their presence in and continuing immigration to California were hotly debated political issues in the late 1890s. In Norris's early work, Mexicans and Chinese are occasionally quaint and picturesque, but on the level of their basic natures, his contribution to the debate was to represent these races as a danger to a California social ethos that has its origin in descendants of a northern Europe immigration.

Although Norris usually expresses this concern for the integrity of the Anglo-Saxon strain in California's racial makeup by means of popular stereotypes—his Latinos, for example, are hot-blooded, his Chinese treacherous[6]—what renders this theme of major interest is that it also rests on several levels of widely shared academic and middle-class belief of his time. The most immediately apparent such level is that present in the title of "A Case for Lombroso." Cesare Lombroso, the late nineteenth-century Italian sociologist, had formulated and popularized a theory about the sources of criminal behavior that he called "Criminal Anthropology." The theory had deeply influenced Émile Zola's portrayal of a murderer in *La Bête Humaine* as well as Norris's portrayal of McTeague in the novel he had begun at Harvard during 1894–95 and that he completed late in 1897.[7] The linchpin of Lombroso's theory was the belief that the criminal was an instance of arrested evolutionary development. Because of a hereditary defect, often the product of alcoholic parents, both a criminal's physical appearance and his behavior were atavistic in nature; that is, he appeared and acted as humans were presumed to have appeared and acted at an earlier stage of evolution. Hence the brutelike physiognomy, proclivity for violence, and amoralism of most criminals. Norris's title "A Case for Lombroso," however, was less an allusion to Lombroso's specific beliefs about criminals than to their adaptation by Max Nordau in his 1895 best-seller *Degeneration*. (Norris signified this debt when he wrote on a clipping of the story, "A subject for Max Nordau."[8]) Nordau's book, which is dedicated to Lombroso, is an attempt to use

Lombroso's ideas to attack several of the major new tendencies in modern artistic expression, including Wagnerian opera, Ibsenite drama, and poetic symbolism. Many modern artists, Nordau believed, exhibit not the physical "stigmata" (Lombroso's term) and atavistic behavior of the "born criminal," but a parallel degeneracy "of a mental order"[9] that is characterized by intense egomania and a consequent absence of an ethical sense. Nordau wrote, "That which nearly all degenerates lack is the sense of morality and of right and wrong. For them there exists no law, no decency, no modesty. In order to satisfy any momentary impulse, or inclination, or caprice, they commit crimes and trespasses with the greatest calmness and self-complacency" (18). They are "morally insane," Nordau continues, a state that is characterized (and now he comes close to describing Cresencia) by "unbounded egotism," "impulsiveness," and extreme "emotionalism" (18–19). It is also of interest that Nordau, in his discussion of Ibsen's heroines (413–15), uses Krafft-Ebing to describe their sadomasochistic relationships and that this account closely resembles the final stages of Stayne and Cresencia's relationship.

Present in Lombroso's and Nordau's ideas and in Norris's story is one of the significant tributaries of the great stream of Darwinian belief during the latter half of the nineteenth century. If evolution was movement forward—first physically in the development of the human species, and then socially in the development of civilization—it was also possible to posit the existence of those who either had failed to progress biologically (as in Lombroso's criminals) or socially (as in Nordau's contemporary artists and Norris's Cresencia) or who shared in both failures (as in Norris's McTeague). Indeed, in one of its most dramatic forms, that of devolution or regression, the theme permitted the sensationalistic depiction of a character regressing before our eyes to an animal state, as in such early Norris works as the short story "Lauth" and *Vandover and the Brute.*

Of course—and this is an important corollary for Norris if not for Lombroso or Nordau—if one accepts the notion of unequal status in the progressive development of the human species, it is not a difficult transition to accept as well that this principle holds for races as well as for individuals—that some races have evolved less successfully than others, both in their physical and moral characteristics, just as is true of specific kinds of criminals and artists, and that it is the duty of the writer both to reflect this truth and to point out the danger of neglecting it. What facilitated in Norris's case the acceptance of racial ideas heavily dependent on an evolutionary notion of human social and moral development is that he had already encountered these ideas on several occasions during his years at Berkeley, where they were offered up as the product of scientific investigation and philosophical probity.

During his junior and senior years at Berkeley (1892–94), Norris took courses from Joseph Le Conte, Charles Mills Gayley, and Bernard Moses, three of the most distinguished University of California professors of that period. From Le Conte he took year courses in geology and zoology, from Gayley a semester course in nineteenth-century poetry and another in literary criticism, and from Moses courses in political economy and Spanish-American history.[10] All of these figures published major works in their fields and had national reputations. Moses is usually credited with founding the discipline of Latin American history, and Le Conte, in addition to his research publications, played a major role in the late nineteenth-century effort by many American scientists to reconcile scientific and religious thought and was later president of the American Association for the Advancement of Science. Le Conte had a medical degree rather than a Ph.D., but Gayley and Moses, as was common for their generation, had doctorates from German universities. What initially attracted Norris to three such diverse academics and their subjects was no doubt their reputation as powerful lecturers. What Norris found in their courses was not only an introduction to the subjects under study but also the commitment of all three, each in his way, to an evolutionary explanation of human development that lent itself to a defense of the concept of racial hierarchies.

Norris was perhaps most deeply engaged by the ideas of Joseph Le Conte, a leading evolutionary theist who had a few years earlier published his major philosophical study *Evolution: Its Nature, Its Evidences, and Its Relation to Religious Thought* (1888). Because I have discussed Le Conte's influence on Norris's basic ideas at some length in my *The Novels of Frank Norris* (1966),[11] I will at this point concentrate on those aspects of Le Conte's beliefs that have a racial implication. In his effort to reconcile evolutionary science and conventional theism, Le Conte posited an evolutionary process in which humans not only have evolved physically under Darwinian principles to their present state but also continue to evolve spiritually toward a full realization of Christian idealism. The presence of a spiritual side in humans, however, does not mean for Le Conte that the physical is to be held in disrespect, as in conventional Christian dualistic belief. Rather, as he explains,

[t]rue virtue consists, not in the extirpation of the lower, but in its subjection to the higher. The stronger the lower is, the better, *if only* it be held in subjection. For the higher is nourished and strengthened by its connection with the more robust lower, and the lower is purified, refined, and glorified by its connection with the diviner higher, and by this mutual action the whole plane of being is elevated. It is only by action and reaction of all parts of our complex nature that true virtue is attained.[12]

Le Conte's belief in the necessary role of the "robust" animal side in human evolution and in man's present nature is constantly echoed by Norris in his defense both of the violence inherent in the Anglo-Saxon Long March and of the still-present instinctive lust for violence in an Anglo-Saxon-bred youth. Norris constantly refers to both ideas throughout his career, but probably seldom as succinctly as in his 1897 *Wave* essay "Ethics of the Freshman Rush," in which he defends the violent behavior present in the annual Berkeley rite: "Fighting is a good thing. We Anglo-Saxons are a fighting race; have fought our way from the swamps of Holland to the shores of the Pacific Coast at an expense of worse things than smashed faces and twisted knees. Civilization is far from the time when the fighting man can be dispensed with. The strongest nations of today are the fighting nations." Fighting, he continues, "wakes . . . that fine, reckless, arrogance, that splendid, brutal, bullying spirit that is the Anglo-Saxon's birthright."[13] In brief, whatever doubts Le Conte himself may have had about the Freshman Rush, it is no far stretch from his explanation of the necessary role of the physical in human evolution and contemporary existence to Norris's application of that explanation to the specific context of the beneficial effects of the Anglo-Saxon Long March and of the continuing Anglo-Saxon strain in American civilization.

It is relevant in relation to Norris's possible adaptation of Le Conte's general ideas into a specific Anglo-Saxon racism to note that Le Conte himself had reached an analogous racist adaptation of evolutionary concepts in his support of the need for the subjugation of Southern blacks. In the course of an 1892 published lecture on "The Race Problem in the South," Le Conte— who was Southern born and educated and who had served the Confederacy as an ordnance official—argued that races evolved at different rates, a condition that resulted in "higher" and "lower" races.[14] In the inevitable "struggle for life and survival of the fittest," a struggle that was "applicable to the races of man also" (359), blacks had found themselves enslaved by their white masters. However, Le Conte felt, this condition had been beneficial to Southern blacks, for their close proximity to white culture had resulted in a gradual advance in their level of civilization. There had been some poor treatment of blacks under slavery, but "[t]he evils were not in the institution, but in its abuses" (361). As for the present, Le Conte argued that blacks should be denied the ballot by any means possible until they had reached a sufficient level of racial maturity.

During Norris's Berkeley years, Charles Mills Gayley was a young man in his early thirties eager to transform the English department (he had been appointed chairman on his arrival in 1889) in accord with the emphasis in

Germanic literary scholarship on the study of literary change as a process akin to evolutionary change in other areas of life. In a clear reference to the role played by German philologists in the application of evolutionary ideas to literary research, Gayley wrote in 1894 that "Scholars in philology . . . have set the new pace by making of their branch a dynamic study: a study of sources, causes, relations, movements, and effects."[15] Thus, he entitled a portion of his course in literary criticism, which Norris took during his senior year, "The Evolution of Literature, and the Differentiation of Literary Species."[16] Hippolyte Taine's immensely influential *History of English Literature* (1859) played a significant role in all literary studies seeking to examine literature in evolutionary terms because his three-part division of the forces behind the production of any literary work—race, milieu, and moment—approximates the interplay of hereditary and environmental factors in physical evolution.[17] And because "race" for scholars of English literature meant the Anglo-Saxon sources of both the English language and a good deal that was distinctive in the English character, and because Gayley himself had a strong interest in Teutonic myth,[18] it appears likely that Gayley's classes indirectly reinforced the Anglo-Saxonism the Norris found more explicitly expressed elsewhere.

The Anglo-Saxon bias of Professor Bernard Moses is far more evident than that which can be inferred for Gayley. Moses's firm belief in the important role of race in a nation's political institutions is revealed by a passage in his *Politics: An Introduction to the Study of Comparative Constitutional Law* (1886):

> The long continuance of a people under any given political order engenders a habit of political thought and action which ripens into a political instinct, and become powerful in determining the form of institutions and the direction of political progress. . . . Thus, the political instincts of a race have their origin in a pre-historic age. . . . It is in [their] force and persistence that we discern the main cause of that tendency displayed in kindred nations to preserve in their governments the essential features of the primitive political institutions of the race to which they belong.[19]

In his lengthy 1887 article "Data of Mexican and United States History," Moses extended this belief in the importance of race in the formation of a nation's institutions to an explanation of the striking difference between the fortunes of the British and Spanish colonies in the Western Hemisphere. The British, in their treatment of the native population, had never "been willing to give up their purity of blood. Since the days of migration from the low lands of Sleswick, the English people, in England, in America, in Australia, have moved steadily and irresistibly forward, and their advance has been marked by the disappearance of the uncultivated aborigines." The Spanish, on the other hand, "have been willing to descend from their European standard of civilization and affiliate with [native tribes] on a lower plane. In Mexico, the Spaniards have mingled their blood with the blood of the natives. . . . The English policy tends to exterminate the barbarians, while, under Spanish dominion, they form a constituent part of the new nation."[20] In brief, in Moses's classes Norris would have found a full and explicit expression of Anglo-Saxon racism, complete not only with the language of "higher" and "lower" civilizations but also with a defense of extreme violence in the preservation of an Anglo-Saxon purity of blood.

Of Norris's seven novels, three—*Vandover and the Brute, McTeague,* and *The Octopus*—have significant and frequently noted anti-Semitic elements. *The Pit* has a few neutral comments about Jews, and Norris's three "popular" novels—*Moran of the Lady Letty, Blix,* and *A Man's Woman*—do not contain any references to Jews. The foundation of Norris's anti-Semitism, as I have suggested, lies in his full and intense commitment to a belief that views other races both as inferior and as a threat to the Anglo-Saxon strain in America's racial makeup. The Jew, because of his assumed physical inferiority, genetic impurity, and undesirable social behavior, is a prominent instance of the threatening racial Other. In dramatizing the Jew in this role, however, Norris also makes use of almost every negative stereotype in traditional anti-Semitic portrayal.

Although *Vandover and the Brute* was published in 1914, it was written for the most part during Norris's 1894–95 year at Harvard, a year during which he also sketched out and wrote a good deal of *McTeague.* The Jewish jewelry salesman Brann appears only in the lengthy section of *Vandover* devoted to a shipwreck off the California coast, while Zerkow the junk collector is present for most of *McTeague.* But the two figures are similar in that both are not only in occupations associated with sharp dealing by Jews but also embody an additional number of stereotypical anti-Semitic characteristics.

Vandover has reached a significant turning point in his life when he undertakes a recuperative voyage from San Francisco to Coronado Island, off San Diego. On his return from Harvard, he had planned a career as an artist, but his pliable and pleasure-seeking nature had also drawn him into "fast" company at the Imperial bar and restaurant and a sexual relationship with the middle-class Ida Wade. His trip to Coronado is prompted by his breakdown after Ida's pregnancy and subsequent suicide. In a sense, Vandover is being educated about life by these experiences as he was not by his Harvard

years. His actions deriving from weakness of character, he should be realizing, have consequences both for others and for himself; the shipwreck on
the return voyage from Coronado is shaped by Norris as a final stage in that
instruction in its dramatization of the vicious struggle for existence at the
heart of all life and thus Vandover's extreme vulnerability if he continues on
his present course.

The Jew Brann plays a prime role in what might be called this last major
effort by experience to instruct Vandover. (Brann is in fact not named until
after Vandover returns to San Francisco; throughout the shipwreck incident
he is merely "the Jew.") Brann is introduced to us: "At supper, the first day
out, a little Jew who sat next to Vandover, and who invariably wore a plush
skull cap with ear-laps, tried to sell him two flawed and yellow diamonds."[21]
Brann is archetypically Jewish in anti-Semitic terms. He is small (Jews were
thought to have been genetically affected by many generations of ghetto
existence), he displays prominent signs of his variant religious beliefs and
practices, and his is an occupation where sharp practices, from selling flawed
goods to outright fraud, are normal and in which he excels.

When the ship runs aground during the night, Vandover's "first impulse
was a wild desire of saving himself; he had not the least thought for any one
else. Every soul on board might drown, so only he should be saved. It was
the primitive animal instinct" (95). As the ship begins to roll over, he catches
sight of Brann, who is transfixed by fear: "he was groveling upon the deck,
huddling a small black satchel to his breast; without a moment's pause he
screamed, 'God 'a' mercy! God 'a' mercy!' . . . Prone upon the deck, his arms
still clasped about his black satchel, the little Jew of the plush cap went into
some kind of fit, his eyes rolled back, his teeth grinding upon each other"
(98, 99). Although Brann is rendered incapable by fear, he is still archetypically Jewish in that the satchel he is grasping contains his diamonds; like
Shylock, in the midst of a crisis threatening his very existence, he thinks of
his "ducats." There are not enough lifeboats. Brann recovers sufficiently to
jump overboard, but the lifeboat he seeks to climb into is full and the ship's
engineer and then all the lifeboat's passengers fight him off. When he persists,
he is beaten by an oar until he is unconscious and drifts off to die. "It was
the animal in them all that had come to the surface in an instant, the primal
instinct of the brute striving for its life and for the life of its young" (103).

The shipwreck incident in *Vandover* is an extreme example of Norris's
melodramatic naturalism and thus, as in most such instances, functions as
a form of allegory. Life, Vandover should and must realize at the conclusion
of the incident, is beneath its veneer of civilized behavior still a struggle for

existence in which the weak do not survive. Although Brann's weaknesses—physical inadequacy, excessive fear, and greed—are not Vandover's, Vandover should have absorbed from his fate the lesson of the danger inherent in weakness. After a brief hiatus of "reformed" behavior on his return, however, Vandover's flawed character again makes itself felt and he begins the process of decline that will bring him to personal dissolution just short of death.

In the context of this study, what is of primary interest in the incident is Norris's choice of a stereotypical Jew to illustrate for Vandover the truth that life is a struggle in which the weak are destroyed. Brann, as I have noted, initially has no name and personality other than that of "the little Jew." Within the dynamics of Norris's racial beliefs, he is thus by definition both physically weak and morally suspect since he is not of Anglo-Saxon stock. Norris did not depict him as Mexican or Chinese (or, for that matter, as Italian or Greek) because the anti-Semitic stereotype of the Jew as dishonestly sharp-minded and physically weak (Fagin, it should be recalled, has Sykes to do his dirty work for him) provided Norris with the best example of the undesirable weakling whom nature weeds out in times of crisis.

It is, however, largely Norris's depiction of Zerkow, the Polish Jewish junk dealer in *McTeague,* that is responsible for his reputation as an anti-Semite. Louis Harap has cited Zerkow as "one of the most anti-Semitic portrayals in American fiction," while Gary M. Levine adds that he is "one of the most loathsome representations in American literature of a Jew."[22] Zerkow's role in the novel, it is generally accepted by commentators on *McTeague,* is to provide an extreme instance of the central theme in the work of the dire consequences of greed in any form. Of the three couples in *McTeague,* Trina is eventually consumed by her lust for gold and McTeague is in part destroyed by its power over him late in the work, while Zerkow and Maria Macapa are driven into insanity by the hold that Maria's dream of a set of gold plates has over them. Even Marcus Schouler, McTeague's friend, is in the end driven to his fate in the desert by a desire to possess Trina's gold.

No one, however, is as much a creature of greed as is Zerkow. In depicting his lust for gold as a pathological state and in also making him a Jew, Norris, as he had in his use of Brann in *Vandover and the Brute,* has slotted a Jew into a specific thematic role in order to take advantage of the anti-Semitic stereotypes associated with that role. Brann, as a Jew, fully illustrates the danger within the universal struggle for existence of the racial weakness attributed to Jews; Zerkow, as a Jew, illustrates the danger of the extreme greed associated with Jews. As I have already noted for Brann, a character from any background could have functioned within these roles, but Norris chose a Jew in both cases because of the close association in his mind between the weaknesses of character and behavior that he wished to represent and the cultural association of the Jew with these weaknesses.

Thus, given his programmatic motivation, and given as well his melo-dramatic tendencies, it is no wonder that Norris produced, when seeking to depict a Jew as the epitome of greed, a portrait close to the surreal in its rendering of a Jew who embodies in a single figure centuries of anti-Semitic representation. Here is Zerkow as he is introduced in the novel:

> Zerkow was a Polish Jew—curiously enough his hair was fiery red. He was a dry, shrivelled old man of sixty odd. He had the thin, eager, cat-like lips of the covetous; eyes that had grown keen as those of a lynx from long search-ing amidst muck and debris; and claw-like, prehensile fingers—the fingers of a man who accumulates, but never disburses. It was impossible to look at Zerkow and not know instantly that greed—inordinate, insatiable greed—was the dominant passion of the man. He was the Man with the Rake, grop-ing hourly in the muck-heap of the city for gold, for gold, for gold. It was his dream, his passion; at every instant he seemed to feel the generous solid weight of the crude fat metal in his palms. The glint of it was constantly in his eyes; the jangle of it sang forever in his ears as the jangling of cymbals.[23]

Many strands of anti-Semitism feed into this account. Zerkow is of course a Shylock in his all-consuming passion for money, but he also alludes to Fagin, in that both he and Dickens's figure function in "the reptilian underworld of the city,"[24] have red hair (attached to the Jew in the Middle Ages as a Sa-tanic symbol), and encourage their underlings—Maria Macapa in Zerkow's case—to commit crimes to increase their wealth.

A more recent and highly popular rendering of the Jew that deeply influ-enced Norris's account of Zerkow was that of Svengali in George's Du Mau-rier's *Trilby* (1894).[25] The novel produced a "Trilby craze," and Norris is known to have at least seen a dramatization of the novel (if he did not also read it) in the spring of 1895,[26] while at Harvard writing a first draft of *McTeague*. Svengali, like Zerkow an eastern European Jew, uses his hypnotic powers to psychologically imprison Trilby and therefore exploit for his own profit her vocal potential, just as Zerkow gradually imprisons Maria in his need to hear her story of the gold plates and has her "perform" it again and again.

Of particular importance in Norris's borrowings from *Trilby* are Zerkow's eastern European origins and his use of a woman to further his greed. As I note several times elsewhere in this study, eastern European Jews were of-ten considered of mixed European and Asiatic blood and therefore prone to physical and psychological degeneracy. (They are the antithesis of the Anglo-Saxon "thoroughbred" heroes of several of Norris's San Francisco *Wave* stories.[27]) Zerkow's "cat-like lips" and eyes like a lynx, and especially his "claw-like, prehensile fingers," a symbol of his preternatural greed, derive in part from his degenerate breeding as a Polish Jew. (Du Maurier's illustrations for *Trilby* also stressed Svengali's prehensile hands.) In addition, both Svengali and Zerkow sexually exploit a non-Jewish woman to satisfy their greed. Indeed, Zerkow's response to gold is deeply sexual at its core, just as Trina's will become. When Maria arrives with gold stolen from McTeague, Zerkow acts like a man anticipating sexual fulfillment. His "eyes glittered on the instant. The sight of the gold invariably sent a qualm all through him; try as he would, he could not repress it. His fingers trembled and clawed at his mouth; his breath grew short" (74). In order to ensure his possession of Maria's story of the gold plates (and thus in his mind the gold itself), he marries her and they have a child who dies soon after birth. Norris's comments at this point bear heavily on the theme of racial degeneracy. Their baby was "a wretched, sickly child, with not even strength enough nor wits enough to cry." It was "a strange, hybrid little being, . . . combining in its puny little body the blood of the Hebrew, the Pole, and the Spaniard" (134–35). The Zerkow–Maria Macapa subplot of *McTeague* thus fleshes out the racial degeneracy themes of "A Case for Lombroso," although now with an explicit anti-Semitic thrust. The animalistic, degenerate eastern European Jew, with his inordinate greed and his capacity to sexually exploit non-Jewish women, reveals the threat posed to an Anglo-Saxon culture by his increasing prominence on the American scene.

The entire novel is indeed permeated, as some commentators have pointed out, with nativist beliefs associated with the Populist movement that was reaching its zenith during the mid-1890s. (Not that Norris is consciously a political nativist; he uses Marcus Schouler to satirize several of the cruder fears of California nativists.) All four of the figures in the novel who come to tragic ends because of hereditary flaws or psychological defects are from non-Anglo-Saxon strains: McTeague is of Irish background, Trina Swiss, Zerkow Polish-Jewish, and Maria Latina. On the other hand, Miss Baker and Old Grannis, who are models of restraint and who have a successful courtship, are of Anglo-Saxon background. In addition, by making in the novel the possession of gold the object of greed and a Jew the principal desirer of gold, Norris appears to be echoing one of the major themes in Populist anti-Semitic rhetoric. True, Zerkow is no British international banker as in that rhetoric, but he is still a Jew lusting after gold, and in the 1890s the allusion to the Populist belief that this equation spelled disaster for American farmers would be hard to miss.

It is tempting to use the word *brilliant* to describe Norris's portrait of Zerkow in *McTeague,* though one would of course be doing so ironically. Norris has managed to combine in the one figure the principal strands both of "classic" anti-Semitism stemming from the Shylock image and of almost all the principal manifestations of the late nineteenth-century resurgence of the prejudice. In his portrayal of a racially degenerate Polish Jew who epitomizes greed, is dishonest, has great psychological powers, and uses a Gentile woman to achieve his ends, Norris gathers up almost all of the various social, theoretical, and political threads making up turn-of-the-century anti-Semitism.

S. Behrman, a major character in *The Octopus,* is never identified by Norris (or by any figure in the novel) as Jewish. It is also problematical whether a Jew played a prominent role in the events leading up to the Mussel Slough Massacre, the armed battle between San Joaquin Valley wheat ranchers and agents of the Southern Pacific Railroad that is the historical event Norris drew upon for the novel.[28] Nevertheless, a number of critics have readily identified Behrman's personal characteristics and thematic role in the novel as distinctively Jewish ("he plainly exhibits the stigmata of the stereotype," Louis Harap has remarked), and Robert Forrey, in his 1975 article, "The 'Jew' in Norris' *The Octopus,*" solidly nailed down the identification.[29]

Behrman, we are told again and again, is grossly fat: "He was a large, fat man, with a great stomach; his cheek and the upper part of his thick neck ran together to form a great tremulous jowl, shaven and blue-grey in colour; a roll of fat, sprinkled with sparse hair, moist with perspiration, protruded over the back of his collar."[30] His obesity plays two significant related roles within the anti-Semitic themes of the novel. First, he is the typical Shylock figure who has fattened himself upon those he exploits. As the principal banker and mortgage holder in Bonneville, he is the usurer par excellence in a land-rich/cash-poor economy, making the farmers of the area pay dearly for the funds necessary to stay afloat. The rancher Osterman, for example, has had to mortgage his crops in advance of harvesting, and Behrman has "squeezed him viciously for interest" (656). But Behrman is also the agent of the P. and S. W. Railroad in the area and has used the monopoly position of the road to "squeeze" the ranchers by manipulating freight rates, requiring shipment to hubs, and inflating costs. These various "sharp practices" are ultimately capped by the P. and S. W. reneging on its seemingly iron-clad agreement to permit the ranchers to buy their land from the railroad at an earlier agreed-upon price. In all of these actions, the ranchers and local farmers uniformly identify Behrman as the man behind the actions. To them, "S. Behrman was the railroad" (630). And here, too, Norris introduces the image of a huge parasite living off the ranchers. Behrman, Harran Derrick exclaims, "has the grip of us and will never let us go till he has squeezed us bone dry" (663).

In both capacities—as moneylender and as the railroad personified—Behrman is imaged as a fat, bloated creature living parasitically on others. This image thus feeds directly into the central image and theme of the novel—that of the corporate power of the railroads sucking dry the farmers of California. Norris makes fully clear this connection between Behrman as a specific Jewish bloodsucker and the railroad in general during a scene in which the ranchers see a large map of the road's California lines.

> The whole map was gridironed by a vast, complicated network of red lines marked P. and S. W. R. R. . . . From Coles, in the topmost corner of the map, to Yuma in the lowest, . . . ran the plexus of red, a veritable system of blood circulation . . . diminutive little blood suckers that shot out from the main jugular and went twisting up into some remote county. . . .
>
> The map was white, and it seemed as if all the colour which should have gone to vivify the various counties, towns, and cities marked upon it had been absorbed by that huge, sprawling organism. . . . It was as though the State had been sucked white and colourless, and against this pallid background the red arteries of the monster stood out, swollen with life-blood, reaching out to infinity, gorged to bursting; an excrescence, a gigantic parasite, fattening upon the life-blood of an entire commonwealth. (806)

Of course, one of the most common and ancient beliefs about Jews is that their tendency to gather in "nonproductive" occupations (banking rather than farming, for example) means that they are parasites upon the community in which they function. In Norris's day, this belief received an emphatic endorsement from midwestern Populists, who—as I discussed in relation to Hamlin Garland's beliefs—frequently viewed English Jewish bankers controlling the mortgages on their land in similar terms. Thus, as I also noted earlier, William H. Harvey's hugely popular Populist tract *Coin's Financial School* (1894) contained a cartoon showing the House of Rothschild as a fat, bloated octopus gathering in the wealth from the nations of the world.[31]

There is obviously little rational logic in the notion that the Jews—that is, S. Behrman as a Jew symbolizing Jewish economic methods and power—were responsible for the events at Bonneville, including the deaths of several of the ranchers. Behrman, after all, as a banker is principally lending other people's money, and as an agent for the railroad is acting on orders from its directors. But in his desire to create a figure who would draw upon a kind of emotional logic to strengthen his fictional portrayal of a villainous agent of social evil, Norris chose a Jew because the cultural climate of the moment offered especially strong support for the belief that it was Jews in particular who were responsible for the farmers' woes. Jews were bloodsuckers, as was the railroad; ergo, it was convincing and "logical" that Behrman be a Jewish railroad agent sucking the blood out of the Bonneville ranchers.

Norris hammers in this logic in one of the major threads of plot in the novel, that involving the relationship between Behrman and Dyke, a hop farmer. Dyke is the polar opposite of Behrman is almost every way. A former locomotive engineer for the railroad, he is skilled at whatever he does but is naive in financial matters. He acquires a mortgage on his homestead from Behrman's bank in order to plant his crop and believes that he has also negotiated a freight rate for its shipment that will permit him a profit. But the rate is raised drastically just before harvest and Dyke goes bankrupt, turns in anger to train robbery, and is apprehended and sent to prison. Dyke, we are assured by Norris, is a good man in the American yeoman vein: he is ambitious and hardworking, loves his daughter, and—as "big-boned, powerful, deep-voiced, good-natured, with his fine blonde beard and massive arms" (744)—is clearly of northern European background.[32] The "contest" between Behrman and Dyke thus plays out on a smaller scale the anti-Semitic thrust of the novel as a whole: the Jew, controlling wealth, cleverly and easily outmaneuvers and defeats the honest, hardworking American "native." Indeed, Behrman manages to escape several attempts on his life in the course of *The Octopus,* including one by Dyke. It is only at the close of the novel that he at last is killed—not by a human force but as the result of accidentally falling into the hold of a ship being loaded with San Joaquin wheat and being suffocated by it. So powerful is Behrman, Norris appears to announce, that it requires a natural force to control and destroy him.

In his portraits of Jews in *Vandover, McTeague,* and *The Octopus* as racially inferior, inordinately greedy, and social parasites, Norris touched base with almost all the major late nineteenth-century American forms of anti-Semitism. The foundation of this prejudice was his full acceptance of the ideology of Anglo-Saxon racial superiority then flourishing in America as a whole and especially among Californians. But Norris also succumbed to the temptation to exploit the reliance on anti-Semitic stereotypes inherent in the ideology to—he believed—strengthen his novels. Anti-Semitism, it should be clear, is not a principal theme in these three novels but rather emerges out of Norris's attempt to provide Vandover with an ignored warning about the operation of natural law, to offer through Zerkow an extreme instance of destructive instinctive behavior, and to objectify the evils of the railroad in a single figure. The anti-Semitism that follows from Norris's mix of ideology and fictional expediency should be recognized for what it is, but its presence should also not preclude a continuing interest in Norris as a richly talented late nineteenth-century American writer.

# 3

# Theodore Dreiser

Dreiser concerned himself fully with the Jewish presence in America only from the mid-1920s to his death in 1945; indeed, it was only in the last decade of that period that he became widely known as an anti-Semite. In addition, although Jews appear occasionally in his writing, they always do so in minor roles, with the single exception of his play *The Hand of the Potter* (1919). Yet despite this seeming paucity of material bearing on Dreiser and the Jews, the subject is both rich and of great interest and importance.[1] From his initial encounters with Jewish merchants in Chicago in the early 1890s to his bitter quarrel with Jewish Hollywood film moguls during the 1930s and '40s, Dreiser interacted vigorously with Jews in a variety of contexts—as employers, friends, editors and publishers, fellow artists and writers, film producers, and so on—and he always had strong feelings, whether negative or positive, about what he believed to be the Jewish element in these encounters. As in several other aspects of a career spanning more than fifty years, Dreiser's beliefs about Jews represent a history in miniature of a significant aspect of early twentieth-century American life—in this instance, that of attitudes toward Jews. In addition, Dreiser's anti-Semitism, when it became a matter of common public assumption in the early 1930s, not only constituted a major challenge to left-leaning intelligentsia of the day—how could a writer, they frequently asked, so preoccupied with aiding the common man also hold such illiberal beliefs?—but also mirrors a still-controversial issue in the study of the many other writers of his generation who shared seemingly irreconcilable racial and social beliefs. The more we know, in short, about Dreiser's anti-Semitism, the greater our insight into a concern present in the interpretation of his generation as a whole.

Dreiser does not mention either in *Dawn* (1931) or *A Hoosier Holiday* (1916), his autobiographies dealing with his Indiana boyhood, any contact with Jews before his arrival in Chicago as a teenager in the late 1880s. It has been common to assume, however, that his later beliefs about Jews can be attributed in part to the anti-Semitism often found during this period both in working-class Catholic homes and western popular belief. Dreiser's father, with his strict Old World Catholicism, may well have held a conventional European peasant distrust of Jews. In addition, farm communities throughout the middle as well as the prairie west were during the 1880s heavily exposed, as I have discussed in connection with Hamlin Garland, to an emerging Populist ideology in which eastern and foreign Jewish bankers controlled the fate of western farmers. Like Sherwood Anderson and Henry Ford, who shared both his middle-west small-town background and his anti-Semitism, Dreiser's childhood environment contained a potent mix of religious and economic ideas antagonistic to the Jews that later served as a foundation for his negative attitudes toward them.

Dreiser's account in *Dawn* of his initial significant encounter with Jews is almost allegorical in its endorsement of the anti-Semitic myth of the Jew as an unscrupulous exploiter of the unwary. In the spring of 1891, just short of twenty, Dreiser was working as a laundry driver in Chicago when he was approached by one of the Jewish owners of a rival company who, "oily" and "ingratiating,"[2] offers him a seemingly far superior position. Dreiser accepts, but once hired finds that the job is very different than promised. Its conditions are more severe, his pay less than indicated, and he is expected to entice customers from his previous employer. In addition, he has an accident for which, though not at fault, he is held responsible. Angry and dismayed, Dreiser decides that

> Jews, for the moment at least, were anathema to me, not so much because they were opposed to me in this instance—though that was not without its import—as that they appeared so sly or clever and withal conscienceless. The morals and trade fairness of the average Gentile as I saw them then—race prejudice, possibly—appeared so much better. Jews, as I then pictured them to myself, were opportunists, with a fine eye for the immediate loophole, regardless of shame, pride, dignity, fairness, anything you will. (563–64)

The stereotype of the Jew as a Shylock-like ruthless urban entrepreneur is here fully expressed. Smooth and ingratiating initially in order to entrap the unknowing, his underlying characteristics of shrewdness, untrustworthiness, and what Dreiser was often later to call "sharp practices" soon emerge.

Sic

However, because Dreiser wrote and revised *Dawn* during the mid-1910s, after his experience of Jews had greatly expanded, he was careful to qualify and therefore in part condemn his earlier characterization in several significant ways. His preference for Gentile businessmen, he admits, may be "race prejudice," and he is at pains to make clear that he has since modified his views, noting that his belief that Jews were opportunists was "as I *then* pictured them" (my italics). He closes the passage with the apologetic remark that "I was not then aware, as I am to-day, of the possible beauty of the individual soul in any race, Jew as well as Gentile" (564).[3]

Dreiser had many occasions to encounter Jews in more favorable circumstances than as exploitative employers in the decade following his late 1910 return to a literary career. He lived during this period in New York—from 1914 to 1919 in Greenwich Village—where he came to know many Jews who were artists, writers, scientists, and intellectuals. Among the most prominent were Abraham Cahan (the founder of the *Jewish Daily Forward* and a novelist of East Side Jewish life), A. A. Brill (Freud's American translator), Jerome Blum (a Chicago artist), Horace Kallen (a philosopher and Judaic scholar), and David Karsner and Mike Gold (left-wing writers). (It is perhaps also worth noting that his mistress from 1913 to 1916 was the actress Kirah Markham, who was half-Jewish.) This was a period of both an increasing Jewish presence in American intellectual and artistic life and of mass immigration of largely impoverished eastern European Jews whose initial home was often on Manhattan's Lower East Side. Dreiser's sympathetic engagement with Jewish life during this phase of his career is signified not only by his acceptance of Jews as intellectual and artistic equals, but also by his composition in 1916 of *The Hand of the Potter,* a tragic play set among Lower East Side Jews.

*The Hand of the Potter,* though written in 1916, was not published until 1919 and not produced until late 1921, and is the only work by Dreiser devoted to a depiction of Jewish life.[4] The play echoes much early twentieth-century Jewish-American fiction and drama in that one of its principal themes is the conflict between immigrant parents and their Americanized children. It is also, however, a striking departure in that Isadore, the oldest son of the thread peddler Aaron Berchansky, suffers from a hormone-induced sexual deviancy that leads him to attack young girls. The central actions of the play are his killing of an eleven-year-old neighbor and his own eventual suicide. This was controversial material in 1916 (H. L. Mencken strongly advised Dreiser against publishing or producing the play), but not because of what might be taken as the author's conscious linking of sexual degeneracy with the Jews. Some later critics, notably Solomon Liptzin,[5] have questioned Dreiser's motives in his setting a story of this kind among East Side immigrants, but this was not an issue raised at the time or for many years afterward. Liptzin and others have also questioned Dreiser's depiction of a Jewish landlord who, Shylock-like, demands his rent in the midst of a family tragedy. Despite these later objections, Abraham Cahan, when he saw the play in 1921, wrote an enthusiastic review in the *Forward* and also wrote Dreiser that "I have seen your play . . . and like it immensely," a response that pleased Dreiser greatly.[6] And Dreiser himself, once the issue of his anti-Semitism became public in the 1930s, offered the play as evidence to the contrary[7] and indeed also claimed that the banning of his books in Germany had arisen from the belief that the author of the play, which had had a successful German production in the 1920s, must be Jewish.[8]

It is understandable that the Nazi belief in Jewish racial degeneracy made post-Holocaust critics especially sensitive to the representation of a "degenerate" Jew. It is equally apparent, however, that Dreiser's intent in the play was not to suggest that Jews are more prone to biological deficiencies than other groups but rather to dramatize the tragic truth that nature is unfair, that it will often strike down the already weak and oppressed, a category of humanity that of course included the East Side Jewish poor now fully evident to Dreiser just a few miles from his lower Manhattan home. Cahan, never one to mince words, addressed the issue of Dreiser's intent in *The Hand of the Potter* head on: "Why," he asked in his *Forward* review, "did Dreiser especially choose a Jewish family to portray such a horrible crime?"[9] One reason, Cahan pointed out, was that Dreiser had based the central action of the play on an actual 1912 crime of this nature involving an East Side Jewish family.[10] In addition, "Dreiser wanted to portray a very poor family and where an American thinks of a very poor New York family there comes to mind the East Side and its poor people."

Indeed, Dreiser's emphasis in the play was above all on the pain of Aaron Berchansky, one of the many fathers in Dreiser's works whose expression of love for his children is thwarted by the circumstances of his life. The emotional climax of the play is not the crime itself but Aaron's soul-wrenching plea to his son, after the crime, that he kill himself. The various other members of the Berchansky family resemble the conventional types of Jewish family drama of the day—one daughter who has married well into an uptown "American" world, another who above all wants a good-time American style, and a son who is anxious to get ahead. The figure who has caused the most anxiety among Jewish critics is that of Isadore's landlord Elkas, who appears only briefly in the last two scenes of the play and who is described by Dreiser as "a small, dark, restless, inquisitive, ferret-like Jew"[11] and who after Isadore's death demands from Berchansky the back rent that Isadore owes him, a sum that includes, as he later points out, the cost of the gas that Isadore used to kill himself. Even Cahan was appalled by this character, and despite his flat statement in his review that Dreiser "is a sincere radical person and is absolutely free of any racism," was also forced to admit, in explaining the presence of Elkas, that "Dreiser is not well-acquainted with Yiddish characters—only what he has heard among Christians, the usual stories and sermons." There is, in short, something of the same intractably irreconcilable mix of conflicting attitudes toward the Jews in *The Hand of the Potter* as in *The Merchant of Venice*. In both plays, the Jew is above all human—he feels anguish and pain as does any human—but he is also Shylock, still practicing his distinctive Jewish wiles. Dreiser's portrayals of Jews at this stage of his career—that is, the late 1910s, when he was writing and revising *Dawn* and writing *The Hand of the Potter*—thus often contains a mixed message, one that Cahan was groping for when he remarked that Dreiser was not a racist but that he also didn't know Jews and Jewish life. Dreiser wished to include Jews among those within the range of his concern and compassion, but he had not shaken loose from the stereotypes that in part denied the applicability of these sentiments to such despicable creatures.

Thus, even during the late 1910s and early '20s, when Dreiser was on the whole sympathetic to the Jewish presence in America, he continued to express the kind of conventional negative stereotype of Jews contained in his response to the Jewish Chicago laundry owner of his youth and in his portrayal of the landlord Elkas. One of his most frequently reprinted anti-Semitic remarks occurred during a 5 November 1922 letter to Mencken, when, on his return to New York after three years in California, he stated that "N. Y. to me is a scream—a Kyke's dream of a Ghetto. The lost tribe has taken the island."[12] To other friends about the same time he wrote that the city had "[t]oo many Jews" and "[t]o [*sic*] many unidealistic Jews."[13] In addition, there is a remarkable consistency throughout Dreiser's career—remarkable in light of his otherwise variable beliefs about the Jews—in his seemingly instinctive turn to the Shylock stereotype when portraying Jews in commercial transactions or roles. I have already noted the Chicago laundry owners and Elkas the landlord, but even in the period of Dreiser's greatest warmth toward Jewish artists and intellectuals, from 1910 to 1925, the stereotype continues to appear in his fiction. In *The Titan* (1914), Isadore Platow, the father of Cowperwood's lover, is described as "a large, meaty, oily type of man—a kind of ambling, gelatinous formula of the male, with the usual sound commercial instincts of the Jews," while the enormously rich Jews who control the international banking firm of Haeckelheimer, Gotloeb and Company are described as "unctuous."[14] And in *An American Tragedy* (1925), when Hortense bargains with Isadore Rubenstein, the son of a store owner, over the coat she is trying to trick Clyde into buying for her, Rubenstein applies a "flattering unction" and also seeks to make clear that a promise of her favors would reduce the price further.[15]

The Shylock stereotype thus appears to be present in Dreiser's mind as a kind of substrata of belief—not so much consciously employed as an ideology (his social ideology during the period before the mid-1920s was usually at odds with the implications of the stereotype) but there nevertheless. Its presence, even in the form of fragmentary remarks in personal letters and brief passages in lengthy novels, may help explain the instability of Dreiser's attitudes toward the Jews because it suggests a core of underlying belief that can come to the surface and dominate his thought when it is activated, as it was to be during the two decades following his 1926 quarrel with Horace Liveright.

Several conditions came together during the early 1920s to ensure that Dreiser and his work were positively received by Jewish critics and readers. By this time, Dreiser had achieved recognition as a major American author. It was thus gratifying to Jews to have a writer of his stature devote an entire work, as no other prominent American novelist had done, to the depiction of immigrant Jewish life. It also did Dreiser's reputation no harm among New York's almost universally left-leaning Jewish intelligentsia that he at this time often adopted Socialist positions and contributed frequently to the Socialist journal *The Call*. The esteem with which Dreiser was held in the Jewish community during this period is suggested by an April 1924 interview with him in *The Day*, a prominent New York Yiddish newspaper, in which most of the interview was given over to Dreiser's questions about Jewish life in New York. The interview concludes, "From the amazingly great amount of information which Mr. Dreiser has about Jewish life in New York, from the subtle points he seems to have gathered from study and observation, together with his power of perception of detail and color, we can expect from him some day the American novel on the Jew in America."[16]

*The Day* interview was among four important interviews that Dreiser gave to Jewish journals during the 1920s—a fact indicative both of the degree of Jewish interest in him during this period and of the cessation of this interest after his remarks during the notorious 1933 *American Spectator* conference on the Jews and the onset of Dreiser's public reputation as a possible anti-Semite. The first, by Berenice Skidelsky, appeared in the Boston *Jewish Ad-*

*vocate* in February 1920 and was soon afterward reprinted in the *New York Jewish News*. Throughout the interview, Dreiser was remarkably positive in his view of the Jewish contribution to American life. Skidelsky reported that Dreiser "declares that the Jews of America are as yeast added to the other ingredients in the nation's making. He sees in them an indispensable leaven for the satisfactory rising and formation of the mass."[17] Their qualities of "warmth," "sweetness," and "love of life" provide them with an intense interest in experience. "They are essentially artists," Skidelsky quotes Dreiser as stating, "transfiguring the commonplace with a glow of hope, and seeing in the hum-drum everyday the stepping-stone to a larger and more vigorous life toward which they are always reaching out." After offering the Lower East Side as an example of these characteristics, Dreiser went on to interpret Jewish business success as above all a triumph of the "imagination." "'The Jew sees possibilities in a nickel,' Dreiser stated, 'which wouldn't be apparent to others in a hundred dollars.' . . . That attitude of mind, or rather of spirit, said Mr. Dreiser, . . . makes for commercial progress, and at the same time it introduces poetry into business." Dreiser went on to note the prominence of Jews in the arts, and then concluded, "All of this direction and achievement is expression of a warm, perfectly legitimate sensuality, inherent in the Jewish temperament, and pregnant with color and vitality. It is an Oriental quality which, infused into the comparative rigidity of the Western peoples, lends them a greater flexibility and thereby offers promise of a richer life."

This extraordinary effusion is of importance for several interrelated reasons. First, Dreiser's remarks constitute an almost point-by-point refutation of the principal anti-Semitic arguments of the period. The Jew is not a vulgar, grasping materialist whose shady commercial practices pollute the national ethos but an artist and poet in all his endeavors.[18] In addition, Dreiser in his interview puts a positive spin on the term "Oriental" in connection with East European Jews. It was widely believed from the 1880s well into the twentieth century by both European and American anti-Semites that East European Jews were racially Asiatic rather than European because of their exposure to Mongol blood, a condition that rendered them both undesirable and unassimilable in European cultures.[19] Dreiser, however, turns this idea on its head; the Jewish characteristics attributable to their "Oriental" heritage are both admirable and capable of being "infused" into Western society. As we shall see, Dreiser almost completely reversed his position on all of these arguments during the 1930s.

Dreiser's rejection of his earlier warm endorsement of the Jewish presence began in the late 1920s; indeed, it is possible to cite an incident in March 1926 as a crucial moment in this reversal. Since 1918, Dreiser had been publishing his works with Boni and Liveright, a firm controlled by Horace Liveright, a New York–born and –educated Jew. Dreiser had initially been attracted by Liveright's willingness to take chances and by his flamboyant and aggressive publishing tactics, but by the mid-1920s he also had begun to doubt his trust-worthiness. All seemed to be made well by the great success of *An American Tragedy*, which Boni and Liveright published in late 1925. The novel received glowing reviews, was a best-seller, and both play and film versions were be-ing planned. Liveright was acting as Dreiser's agent in connection with these adaptations, and for the movie version had begun negotiations with Jesse L. Lasky, head of Famous Players–Lasky film company. W. A. Swanberg, in his *Dreiser* (1965), and Tom Dardis, in his *Firebrand: The Life of Horace Liver-ight* (1995), have recounted at considerable length the complicated story of Dreiser's and Liveright's unspoken and usually false assumptions about their agreement on how much was to be asked for the film rights and about what was to be Liveright's agent's share for the sale. It is therefore only necessary here to specify Dreiser's interpretation of what occurred at the infamous meeting involving Dreiser, Liveright, and Lasky at the Ritz Hotel in March 1926, when Liveright accused Dreiser of being a liar and Dreiser threw a cup of coffee in his face and stormed out of the meeting. Because Liveright had initially indicated that $35,000 was the highest he thought Lasky would offer for the rights, but since Lasky when pressed was in fact willing to pay $80,000 as Dreiser's share, Dreiser believed that Lasky and Liveright, who were old friends, had conspired in advance of the meeting to offer Dreiser the lower price.[20] Liveright's agent's share would be much less at this price, but Lasky would more than make up that loss. Although Dreiser did not mention in his various accounts of the incident that Lasky and Liveright were Jews, it is not difficult, especially in relation to his later comments on unscrupulous Jews in the movie and publishing businesses, to see him construing the incident as a repetition of the archetype of Jewish sharp dealing he had encountered in Chicago. Here again the unknowing and trusting country boy was being set up as a patsy by conniving urban Jews.

Indeed, Dreiser's belief that the deal with Famous Players–Lasky was tainted by underhandedness involving Jews received confirmation, he be-lieved, by a revelation several years later concerning the 1926 contract he signed with the company. Lasky failed to produce a silent film version of *An American Tragedy*, but in mid-1930, Paramount (the successor of Famous Players–Lasky) became interested in a talkie version. Dreiser, however, be-lieved that his original sale of the rights covered only a silent film, and he wrote the New York lawyer Theodore Kiendl on 18 August 1930 requesting an opinion.[21] In the course of this letter, Dreiser noted that before agreeing to Lasky's terms in 1926, he had consulted with Louis Levy, a lawyer with Chadbourne, Stanchfield, and Levy, a firm that had represented him earlier. It was only later that he discovered that the firm also had a business relationship with Famous Players–Lasky and that the terms of the contract endorsed by Levy were, Dreiser believed, therefore biased in favor of Famous Players. Again, as with the original sale, there appeared to be a conspiracy involving Jews to cheat Dreiser.

It is therefore not surprising that Dreiser's final two interviews with Jewish journals, in February 1929 and June 1930, have a very different cast than those of the early 1920s. In the first, "Dreiser Looks at the Russian Jews," Sulamith Ish-Kishor questioned Dreiser, who had made a highly publicized journey to the Soviet Union a year earlier, about the condition of Russian Jews. Most Jews in the Soviet Union are unhappy, Dreiser responded, because the communist economic system does not permit full expression of their talents as "natural-born traders. . . . The Jews are natural-born traders [he repeats]; for centuries they've been acting as go-betweens. . . . It may be something biologically, ethnically, even—who knows—psycho-genetically predestined." Russia contains "many idealistic Jews who study all the time and never make a cent," Dreiser admits, "but they're not the active members of the race, the ones you encounter everywhere."[22] This distinction between the Jew as rarely encountered idealist and as omnipresent natural-born trader is reflected in the interview itself, since Dreiser has very little to say about Russian Jews as artists and intellectuals—that is, as the possible "yeast" in Soviet culture—but rather devotes almost all his attention to the ineradicable "trader" qualities of Jews that make the "race" unassimilable within contemporary Russian society. Dreiser, in brief, has moved from a consideration of the Jew founded on the Jewish aptitude for the life of the mind and spirit (the capacity for "imagination," "poetry," and a "richer life" he attributed to Jews in 1920) to one that stressed an instinctive compulsion to engage in profitable commerce.

Dreiser's final interview on the Jews, "Theodore Dreiser Discounts Intermarriage," appeared in the San Francisco *Jewish Journal* in June 1930, when he was in the city to visit the imprisoned radical Tom Mooney. Although the interview, by Raymond Dannenbaum, covers a variety of topics, it is united by Dreiser's contempt for many Jewish assumptions and beliefs, a contempt that often reflects traditional anti-Semitic attitudes. Jews don't really support Zionism, he begins, because "[y]ou want to be everywhere like gypsies. You want to be a race which envelops the earth. You'd like to have your fingers in every pie"[23] (the pushy Jew). Jews are "neurotically conscious of opposition" (the oversensitive Jew). "You're in the forefront of every movement, and yet you keep shouting for a lift" (the Jew asking for special favors). "The Jew an eternal defender of Justice? Bunk! Jews have always crybabied about Justice, but what they want is Justice for themselves—a special and particularly pro-Jewish Justice. That's not Justice!" (again the Jew as self-centered special pleader). "Jews *invented* commerce. . . . And your great Jewish banking firms. Don't they move the wheels of commerce today?" (the Jew as International Banker, controlling world trade).

It is of interest that this interview with its anti-Semitic tone appeared at the onset of the 1930s, a decade marked by a significant increase in American anti-Semitism. On the national scene, the deepening depression heightened the traditional use of the Jew as scapegoat. Henry Ford and others had found new "evidence" during the early 1920s in the *Protocols of the Learned Elders of Zion* forgery for the conspiratorial theory of Jewish world domination, and during the 1930s, various nativist and fascist groups continued to spread the message that the Depression had been caused by international Jewish bankers.[24] The prominence of the Nazi party in German politics during the late 1920s and early '30s, climaxed by Hitler's coming to power in early 1933, gave exposure and credibility to virulent anti-Semitic ideas and practices. And throughout the United States, the earlier often sporadic and tacit exclusion of Jews from social and educational institutions became a more widespread and openly expressed policy.[25]

Given this tendency in society at large and given the drift in his own beliefs during the 1920s, Dreiser probably did not need any further stimulus toward a more pronounced anti-Semitism during the 1930s. But if he did, his further difficulties with Paramount in 1931 about the filming of *An American Tragedy* would have provided it. To tell a long and complicated story briefly (it takes Swanberg more than five pages to narrate it), after Dreiser signed a contract for a sound version of the novel in early January 1931, a script was quickly prepared by writer Samuel Hoffenstein, and the movie, directed by Josef von Sternberg, was put into production. The contract specified that Dreiser could review the script and make suggestions for change but that Paramount had the power to make the movie it wanted to. Dreiser did object vehemently to the script because it omitted almost all of the novel's social themes in favor of its love story and crime elements, but Paramount went ahead with its version. Dreiser then persuaded a group of New York intellectuals to attend an advance showing of the movie; when this group agreed with his judgment, he unsuccessfully sought to persuade a court to issue an injunction against its distribution.

In all, this scenario took almost half a year to play out, from January to mid-summer 1931, with Dreiser at the end believing that his work had been perverted by a Hollywood company far more interested in profits than in preserving the integrity of a major work of art. Although Dreiser did not at this time specifically cite himself as the victim of a group of unscrupulous Jews, it is hard to believe that the thought was not there. The same company that had attempted to cheat him in 1926 was at the center of the controversy. It was still headed by Lasky, and indeed Liveright had joined it as a producer in the summer of 1930. And the major figures in determining the shape of the movie adaptation, Hoffenstein and von Sternberg, were both Jews.

In addition, in the years that followed this incident, the specific target of Dreiser's anti-Semitism was often the film industry, which was of course dominated by Jews in every phase of ownership and production. Dreiser expressed a characteristic example of this animus in May 1933, when he wrote a cautionary letter to Sherwood Anderson on how to deal with Hollywood film companies. Always get everything in writing, Dreiser advised.

> Next, in connection with any contract offered you, in the first place avoid signing it until you have had a chance to study it and, furthermore, to have an American lawyer, not a Jewish one, examine the contract for you. Do not take the statement or the paper of any lawyer representing any Hollywood proposition without first turning it over to your own lawyer—always an American—with a view to getting yourself straight.
>
> If you do not do these things, you will probably find that you have let yourself in for complete defeat in whatever it is you wish to do.[26]

Having been "taken" not only in his youth by Chicago laundry owners but more recently by their descendants, Hollywood film moguls, Dreiser is advising another village-bred midwesterner to be wary.

Dreiser's increasing irritation with certain aspects of the Jewish presence in America did not receive widespread attention until the early and mid-1930s, when he "went public" in spectacular fashion. He had become one of the founding editors (along with Ernest Boyd, George Jean Nathan, Eugene O'Neill, and James Branch Cabell) of the *American Spectator,* a tabloid literary monthly that published its initial issue in November 1932. From the first, Dreiser believed that the journal should also deal with serious social concerns, while Boyd and Nathan, who were its managing editors, were for maintaining a lighter note. Something of this division appears in the "Editorial Conference (With Wine)" that appeared in the September 1933 issue.[27] The four editors other than Dreiser sought to bring a comic and even burlesque tone to their discussion of the conference's topic of the Jew in America. (Cabell's contribution was that the Jewish problem could be solved by awarding American Jews the state of Kansas.) Dreiser, however, was uniformly substantive and somber in his remarks. His "quarrel" with Jews, he stated, was that the Jew was "really too clever and too dynamic in his personal and racial attack on all other types of persons and races." Given their aggressive shrewdness, Jews tend to take over certain occupations and indeed entire nations. In the course of the discussion, Dreiser offered several possible responses to this problem. Jews could be limited in number in professions such as law or they could be encouraged to establish their own nation. Dreiser also presented for discussion the belief of "a distinguished Jewish friend," whom he does not name, that the Jew "be left just as he is, persecuted if you please, Hitlerized or pogromed or socially discriminated against, but left to work out his fate according to his present circumstances and handicaps or advantages, as you will." The basis for this view is that because Jews drift to where they can "share in and take advantage" of what nations have to offer, they are always outsiders and as such can expect to be persecuted.

Dreiser's statements in the conference, both his and those he attributes to a friend, support the traditional anti-Semitic view that it is the Jew himself, because he is so aggressive and shrewd in his pursuits (the conventional image of the Jew as "pushy" and as committed to "sharp practices"), who is to blame for being persecuted and for being severely restricted in the range of his activities. This idea was especially disturbing in relation to events of the early 1930s. European and American fascist organizations had been increasingly open throughout that period in their call for the "control" of Jews by both legislation and violence, and in January 1933 this position appeared to receive major validation by Hitler's assumption of power in Germany. Dreiser may have thought he was distancing himself from remarks that fail to condemn social discrimination, pogroms, and Hitler's promise to curb the role of the Jew in Germany by attributing them to someone else, but even to introduce them seriously into the discussion was provocative and foolhardy because they suggest that one way to settle the problem of the stateless, leechlike Jew in America was to leave him to his own fate at the hand of anti-Semitic mobs.

Dreiser was in fact aware of the incendiary character of his comments. He wrote to George Jean Nathan on 26 May 1933, shortly after the conference took place: "This editorial conference article cannot go through without a final o. k. from me, as well as an o. k., of course, from the other editors. It involves statements and a point of view which, coming from me, are sure to have national reactions and we will have to be careful of the language. I want to o. k. all my remarks in specific detail."[28] It is difficult to gauge "national reactions," but the article was widely commented upon and also received one response in particular, that by Hutchins Hapgood, which was eventually to provide Dreiser with widespread notoriety as an anti-Semite.

Hapgood was an old friend from Dreiser's years as a Greenwich Village resident during the 1910s. Though not a Jew, he had made his literary reputation with *The Spirit of the Ghetto* (1902), a work sympathetically depicting East Side Jewish life. Hapgood wrote initially on 4 October, addressing his letter to the editors of the *American Spectator* and also not naming any individual conferee in the letter itself. His basic point was that he expected better of a "liberal" journal than an article that appeared to endorse, at this particular moment in history, popular prejudices against the Jews. He also expressed the Marxist position that anti-Semitism obscured a realization of the centrality of class warfare in the modern world. "The legitimate struggle today is between groups divided on economic policy and interests. Other points of struggle—national, racial and religious—are throwbacks and barbaric remnants, and so obscuring and harmful."[29]

Hapgood appears to have written with the expectation that his comments would be published by the *Spectator* as a letter to the editor. Instead, Ernest Boyd responded briefly to Hapgood and then turned over Hapgood's letter to Dreiser, who responded at length on 10 October. Hapgood then replied to Dreiser on 18 October, and on 28 December Dreiser answered. Hapgood then closed the correspondence with a letter to Dreiser on 28 February 1934. The more formal context and therefore more restrained tone both of Dreiser's published conference comments and of Hapgood's initial letter to the editors thus gave way to the greater directness and openness of a personal correspondence between two old friends, and it is this portion of the exchange— Hapgood's second and third letters and Dreiser's replies to Hapgood's first and second letters—that Hapgood published in the *Nation* on 17 April 1935.[30] It is not known why Hapgood waited a year and a half before he published the correspondence. A likely explanation, however, is that the tide of anti-Semitism throughout the world and in Europe in particular had increased even further and that he eventually felt compelled to help expose its dangers in whatever way he could.

It is not necessary to discuss Hapgood's letters other than to comment that he pulled no punches when he commented in his brief introduction to the correspondence that he was "horrified and astonished" by Dreiser's initial letter of 10 October (436) and when he noted in his own letter of 18 October that Dreiser's letter was a "clear expression . . . of anti-Semitism" and that if Dreiser "hadn't signed the letter I might have thought that it was written by a member of the Ku Klux Klan or a representative of Hitler" (437). To realize what disturbed Hapgood so greatly, it is necessary to isolate Dreiser's key points because his two long letters are characteristically Dreiserian in the sense that they diffusely cover much tangential ground.

Dreiser's diagnosis of the Jewish problem contains the familiar charge, though now stated by him more vehemently than ever before in a public forum, that Jews gather principally in the professions and commerce and that their behavior in these areas is suspect. In the most often quoted passage from Dreiser's letters to Hapgood, he charged that "they are not the day laborers of the world—pick and shovel; they are by preference lawyers, bankers, merchants, money-lenders and brokers, and middlemen. If you listen to Jews discuss Jews, you will find that they are money-minded, very pagan, very sharp in practice, and, usually, in so far as the rest is concerned, they have the single objective of plenty of money" (436). Dreiser also argued that the Jew, whatever nation he inhabits, remains principally a Jew, that "he maintains his religious dogmas and his racial sympathies, race characteristics, and race cohesion as against all the types or nationalities surrounding him wheresoever" (436). In brief, his diagnosis is that the Jew possesses undesirable racial characteristics and that there is little hope that these will be diminished by assimilation.

Dreiser, however, also provides a remedy—that Jews establish a nation of their own, one where their distinctive characteristics would not stimulate an inevitable anti-Semitic reaction. The Zionist movement had, of course, been active for many years in promoting the idea of a Jewish return to a Palestinian homeland, but Dreiser suggests that any portion of the world will do. The weakness in the German response to the Jewish problem, he implies, is not in their analysis of it but in their substituting the "barbarism" of their persecution of German Jews for a planned resettlement elsewhere.[31] Thus, although Dreiser at this point, as indeed as he was to do for the remainder of his life, criticizes the Nazi mistreatment of Jews, his own analysis of the origin of the Jewish "problem" differs little in its basic thesis from Hitler's racist ideology that the Jew is an undesirable and unassimilable presence within a nation and that he must be dealt with accordingly.

Dreiser's published correspondence with Hapgood caused much consternation, nowhere more than among Communist Party leaders. Although not a member of the party, Dreiser had been a valuable supporter of many of its endeavors and positions since the early 1930s. His argument with Hapgood, however, was disturbing to Communists both because many Jews were party members, especially in New York, and because Dreiser's basic position contradicted official party ideology that social problems stemmed primarily from differences in class and wealth and that anti-Semitic beliefs both obscured this truth and were a means of maintaining control of the masses by an oligarchy. Soon after the *Nation* article appeared, Dreiser was asked to visit the offices of the *New Masses* to receive instruction on this matter; when this meeting did not reach a satisfactory conclusion, a group of party stalwarts visited Dreiser, following which the *New Masses* on 30 April 1935 published an article entitled "Dreiser Denies He Is Anti-Semitic."

The unsigned article is devoted to a point-by-point refutation of Dreiser's argument, to a restatement of Lenin's position regarding the Jews, and to the representation of the Soviet Union as an ideal state for Jews. Its principal interest is the writer's report of the possible origin of Dreiser's beliefs about Jews, that "[a]t the second meeting with the larger group, Dreiser obviously reflected experiences he had with some Jewish lawyers and some Jewish businessmen. He said that in his dealings with them he had met with sharp practices, and this without doubt accounted for his discriminating views in his letters."[32] Dreiser's own words appear only in the form of "Dreiser's Statement" of about 100 words, in which he denied that he made no distinction between the Jewish workingman and the Jewish capitalist and in which he repudiated any possible use of his letters by Nazi propagandists. "I have no hatred for the Jew," he wrote, "and nothing to do with Hitler or fascism."[33] Although Dreiser apparently wished to make peace with the party and its leaders, he also was not willing to alter his basic beliefs either about the nature of the Jewish presence in America or about the best way to meet the challenge provided by that presence. All he was willing to do, it would appear, was to deny that intense feelings underlay his beliefs and to reject their relationship to events on the world stage.

Mike Gold, the feisty Communist journalist, seems to have recognized that Dreiser was retracting very little, if anything, of the Hapgood exchange. A week after the appearance of "Dreiser Denies He Is Anti-Semitic" in the *New Masses,* he published in the same journal "The Gun Is Loaded, Dreiser!"—an article reflecting his personal bitterness over Dreiser's views.[34] It had been Gold who had shepherded Dreiser around the East Side years earlier when Dreiser was gathering impressions for *The Hand of the Potter* and in so doing had revealed to Dreiser a world of Jewish poverty and misery. Because Gold devoted almost all his article to further instructing Dreiser in Marxist beliefs regarding the Jews, his piece is of interest primarily for its illustration of his struggle to reconcile the Dreiser who was a great artist and who had fought against oppression of the working class and the Dreiser who expressed anti-

Semitic beliefs. This was not an easy task, as many have found who faced an analogous effort in relation to other twentieth-century writers, and Gold's solution to the problem is weak and unsatisfactory. Dreiser has anti-Semitic views, he decides, but at heart is not an anti-Semite. And, following up on the title of his piece, Dreiser is like a child with a loaded gun; he may cause immense harm with the weapon, but he is not guilty of evil intent.

These efforts by the party to cleanse Dreiser of his anti-Semitic beliefs were to no avail. On 27 June 1935, less than two months after Gold's article, Dreiser wrote his Russian friend Sergei Dinamov, "Apart from what I said to the group representing the new *Masses,* I have not changed my viewpoint in regard to the Jewish programme in America. They do not blend as do the other elements in this Country, but retain as they retain in all countries, their race solidarity and even their religion—here particularly. . . . You saw one result of their peculiar race drift in their management of the Movies in this Country."[35]

During the early and mid-1930s, as Dreiser's ideas about the "peculiar race drift" of the Jews were bringing him an unwanted criticism and notoriety, his experience with film companies and publishers appeared to further confirm his position. He came to believe that Universal Studios, headed by Carl Laemmle, Jr., a Jew, had plagiarized his *Jennie Gerhardt* in its 1932 film version of Fannie Hurst's popular novel *Back Street,* and beginning in 1935 he pursued this claim over several years in angry correspondence with Universal and through various lawyers.[36] Horace Liveright, Inc., had failed in early 1933, and in 1934 Dreiser signed a contract with Simon and Schuster for the publication of all his earlier and forthcoming works. The relationship soon soured, however, on much the same grounds as with Liveright—that is, Simon and Schuster wanted him to produce a promised novel, and Dreiser felt it was stinting on support of his other efforts. Indeed, by the late 1930s he also was claiming that the firm had cheated him by the way it had disposed of copies of his Liveright books that it had acquired. In a letter of 6 May 1939 to his longtime friend and agent William C. Lengel, Dreiser outlined his case against Simon and Schuster, both of whom were Jewish, and then went on to connect what he held to be their shabby and even dishonest treatment of him with

> this constant under-cover talk about my anti-Judaism which consisted of the mild correspondence I once had with Hutchins Hapgood, [which] has caused all sorts of people who are inimical to me—writers and what not—to not only play this up but exaggerate it in every quarter, so that I feel that Simon and Schuster may themselves be joined with this issue to the end of taking me off

the market entirely. It may be that they identify me with Germany and have decided to include me in their campaign against Teutonic Culture.[37]

Writing from Los Angeles to his New York acquaintance Dayton Stoddart a few days later, on 10 May, he asked Stoddart to "get me the names of fairly recently organized non-Jewish publishers. I am thinking of changing from Simon and Schuster."[38]

During this last phase of his career Dreiser continued to speak out publicly against Nazi persecution of the Jews while expressing privately, in correspondence with friends, anti-Semitic beliefs. In 1939, for example, he contributed to the League of American Writers publication *"We Hold These Truths": Statements on Anti-Semitism by 54 Leading American Writers, Statesmen, Educators, Clergymen and Trade-Unionists.* Yet to Stoddart he wrote on 22 June 1939 from Los Angeles that "[t]he movies are solidly Jewish. They've dug in, employ only Jews with American names and buy only what they cannot abstract & disguise. And the dollar sign is the guide—mentally & physically. That America should be led—the mass—by this direction is beyond all believing. In addition they are arrogant, insolent, and contemptuous."[39]

And to H. L. Mencken on 3 October 1939, not long after the German invasion of Poland and the outbreak of World War II, he wrote, "I begin to suspect that Hitler is correct. The President may be part Jewish. His personal animosity toward Hitler has already resulted in placing America in the Allied Camp—strengthening Britain's attitude and injuring Germany in the eyes of the world. The brass!"[40] Indeed, in the light of these comments, even Dreiser's contribution to the League of American Writers' collection of statements opposing anti-Semitism appears excessively cautious and self-defensive. Dreiser places the persecution of the Jews in a larger context of the persecution of minorities throughout the world, naming Germany and its Jews only once and Hitler not at all. He devotes his final paragraph to the issue of what the "equitable individual" can do to contribute to the "abolishment of these outrages" and states that he himself can do no more than speak out, as "the record of my personal appeals over many years" proves. He concludes, petulantly, "What more would you have me say or do?"[41]

Dreiser's anti-Semitic beliefs were no doubt acquired in the homes, streets, and schoolyards of the small Indiana towns of his youth. He then found the mythic Shylock characterization of the Jew as shrewd, mercenary, and untrustworthy in business matters confirmed by his early encounters with Jews in Chicago. After a period of goodwill toward Jews fostered by friendships with and admiration of Jewish artists and intellectuals, his earlier beliefs were reconfirmed by dealings with Jewish lawyers, publishers, and film moguls, most of whom he believed to be unscrupulous. He also began to reflect, from the late 1920s onward, the anti-Semitic belief that Jews were both an undesirable and unassimilable element within American society.

Dreiser is not the only American writer to succumb to the widespread anti-Semitism of this period, whether its sources were those of rural ignorance and fear or of racist-based "historical" demonstration. And there is no doubt that he was victimized by Jews on some occasions in business dealings from the late 1920s onward. Unlike many other American writers and intellectuals of his generation who harbored traces of anti-Semitism, however, Dreiser refused to modify these beliefs during the 1930s, when it came to be realized that the former almost reflexive anti-Semitism both of polite society and of working-class America contained a deadly political dimension.

It is not as though Dreiser did not have precise instruction on the danger of his beliefs during this decade from his many admirers who were deeply chagrined by them. This instruction usually was along two lines, one of which is illustrated by an exchange between Dreiser and Ernest Boyd, an urbane literary critic and friend with whom Dreiser was later to collaborate in the editing of the *American Spectator*. At a dinner party given by Boyd in late April 1931, just a month or so after Dreiser's confrontation with Liveright and Lasky over the sale of the film rights of *An American Tragedy*, Dreiser, without realizing that one of the guests was Jewish, made anti-Semitic remarks about Jews in show business. After he wrote to Boyd on 1 May apologizing for introducing "TNT" into the occasion,[42] Boyd replied that his own point of view was that "Gentiles, trying to run the same racket today, have to and do adopt the same methods. If Hollywood, for example, were controlled by Gentiles but aimed at the same audience and profits, it would be just the same as we see it. Mass production and excess profiteering produce the same results in Jew and Gentile."[43] Dreiser, however, despite Boyd's not uncommon perception, was never able to make the leap from conclusions based on his own personal experience to those derived from a wider perspective. Jews had treated him shabbily and therefore it was their Jewishness, not the social context in which they functioned, that was to blame.

The second major kind of instruction that Dreiser failed to respond to centered on the danger inherent in his remarks. In his 1 May letter to Boyd, Dreiser wrote, after noting his friendships with a number of Jews, "Nevertheless, I reserve the right to pass criticism on the actions of any portion of any race that I consider detrimental or offensive to me." This reliance on the seeming unassailability of one's personal opinion perhaps had some validity in 1931, but not in 1935, with Hitler firmly in power and with a rabid anti-Semitism rampant throughout the fascist movements of Europe and America, as Dreiser was frequently told—not by his detractors but by his friends and supporters. Hapgood, the *New Masses,* and Gold repeated several times in their 1935 articles on Dreiser's anti-Semitism that his beliefs strongly resembled those of the Nazis and other fascist organizations. For a major American author so strongly identified with the ideals of social justice to express such beliefs was not only a betrayal of those ideals—and hence Hapgood's and Gold's obvious anger—but also an extraordinary failure of political imagination. "I am an individual," Dreiser told the *New Masses* delegation. "I have a right to say what I please."[44] What Dreiser failed to comprehend was that in the context of the mid-1930s and the specific subject of the Jews, he was not only an individual but also the world-famous author Theodore Dreiser. His ideas in this volatile area carried resonance and weight, and it was therefore necessary for him to accept responsibility for their impact rather than to retreat into the bastion of "personal opinion."

Dreiser's great works had been written by the time his more pronounced anti-Semitism emerged in the late 1920s. He nevertheless remained for the two post–*American Tragedy* decades of his life a major presence on the American cultural scene. There are many strands in that presence, some estimable, some less so, with his anti-Semitism one of the latter.

# 4

## Edith Wharton and Willa Cather

A study of Edith Wharton's and Willa Cather's attitudes toward Jews requires a somewhat different approach than that which was employed for the figures already discussed. Each woman succeeded in keeping much of her private life and opinions out of public knowledge during both her lifetime and afterward. Wharton's affair with Morton Fullerton was not revealed until several decades after her death, and the editors of her letters, R. W. B. and Nancy Lewis, refused to publish those that expressed the blatant anti-Semitism of her later years. Cather's lengthy relationships with other women also led her to be secretive about her personal life, and she included a provision in her will prohibiting the publication of her letters.[1] There is little available from their careers, in other words, similar in its openness of expression to Dreiser's frank letters and interviews, Norris's essays on a variety of subjects, and Garland's diaries and autobiographies.

Wharton's and Cather's fictional expression of their attitude toward Jews also differs from that of these other writers. Dreiser lacks a novel dealing extensively with Jews, although he frequently portrays them in minor roles, and they seldom appear at all in Garland's fiction. Norris includes major Jewish characters in three of his novels, but the novels themselves, as I have argued, have central themes independent of their Jewish characters. Wharton and Cather vary from these figures in that in addition to having produced a number of relatively minor novels and stories containing Jews, each also wrote a major novel in which not only is a Jew a principal character but the issue of the Jew in American life also constitutes a central theme in the work. *The House of Mirth* (1905) and *The Professor's House* (1925) are richly nuanced examinations of the Jewish presence in America and thus occupy a central position in the study of their author's attitude toward the Jews lacking in any one novel by Dreiser, Norris, and Garland.

Edith Wharton came by her patrician distaste for Jews almost as inevitably as her heroine Lily Bart came by her taste for the comforts and luxuries that money can buy—that is, it was bred in her bones by birth and upbringing. Wharton stemmed from two of New York's oldest and most socially prominent families, made a formal debut, married well, and, before she became a writer, divided her time between the New York "season" and New England resorts. She came to maturity within a climate of unacknowledged custom and unspoken belief that (as she brilliantly depicted in *The Age of Innocence*) nevertheless encapsulated those within it in rigid codes of value and action. Wharton was later to rebel against these codes insofar as they thwarted the expression of the felt life and inhibited a woman's freedom to live as freely as a man might, but she was never able, as is also true of almost all her New York and Boston fellow writers of her own class and background, to divorce herself from the patrician fear of the Outsider represented by the Jew.

Indeed, from a patrician point of view there was good reason during the early decades of the twentieth century to believe that the barbarians were at the gates. Their assault had come in two waves—the largely Germanic Jewish immigration of the pre–Civil War period followed by the vast numbers of eastern European Jews, beginning in the 1880s and not ceasing until the restrictive immigration laws of the early 1920s. From a patrician view, each of these groups constituted its own kind of threat to American society. By the early twentieth century, when Wharton came on the scene, Jews of Germanic background were usually second-generation Americans. A number of them derived from families that had made fortunes in retailing and banking (the Seligmans, Altmans, Bloomingdales, Lehmans, Goldmans, Kuhns, Loebs, etc.) and that had also made inroads into society by means of philanthropic and political activities.[2] But there was also now on the scene the recently arrived, poor, and seemingly unassimilable East European Jews who occupied squalid ghettoes from Boston to Baltimore. Speaking little English, confined principally to peddling and the needle trades, fiercely eager to push ahead economically and thus seemingly unaware of any other values, they appeared very much a threat to a social class that prided itself on modes of behavior and expression derived from long-proven standards of taste and decorum. No wonder, then, that figures of Wharton's generation such as Henry Adams, Henry James, and Henry Cabot Lodge, who shared her East Coast patrician background, also shared her dismay at this encroachment and thus the possible corruption of their civilization by an alien race. This sentiment varied in expression from Adams's and Lodge's open anti-Semitism to James's perplexity and bewilderment, as revealed in *The American Scene* (1906), when, after a twenty-year absence from New York, he encounters the strange hordes that had overrun his once-familiar world.

As has often been pointed out, many well-to-do second- and third-generation Germanic-American Jews viewed the new immigration as a threat to their own social aspirations. Indeed, one can see the basis for this resentment clearly in the portrayals of Simon Rosedale in *The House of Mirth* and Louie Marcellus in *The Professor's House*. Both Rosedale and Marcellus are thoroughly Americanized Jews who are also wealthy men with cultural interests; no trace of the ghetto is apparent in either their known origins or current way of life. Nevertheless, although there is little, it would seem, to be feared in such men, a major thematic function of their Jewishness is to indicate the danger posed by a commercial ethic to traditional beliefs and ways of life. Of course, the wealthy international Jewish banker of populist rhetoric played a similar role; the Shylock stereotype transcends wealth and class, as is apparent by his appearance in figures ranging in social status from Norris's S. Behrman to Dreiser's Elkas the landlord. The image was reenergized at the turn of the century by the millions of recently arrived Jews whose presence provided a powerful fresh basis for its acceptance. The fear that these totally alien ghetto Jews, driven by their powerful desire to gain what the New World had to offer, would overrun and take over a rich culture developed over the centuries thus shapes the portrayal of all Jews, whatever their origin or nature. The barbarian is at the gate, in brief, even if he wears a London-made suit and can discuss the opera.

Wharton was educated at home and by tutors, and it was only after her marriage in 1885, when she was in her early twenties, that she discovered the world of new ideas stimulated by the mid-century Darwinian revolution in thinking about human origin and nature. As she wrote in a well-known passage in her autobiography *A Backward Glance* (1934), she was led by a family friend to the works of Charles Darwin, Alfred Wallace, Herbert Spencer, and other "popular exponents of the great evolutionary movement" and found in them "an overwhelming sense of cosmic vastnesses which such 'magic casements' let into our little geocentric universe."[3] Although she does not go on to discuss what specific ideas she absorbed from this body of writing about the relation of evolution to interpretations of contemporary social life, it is possible to see in her later work evidence of two broad streams of her engagement in evolutionary belief.

The first is her often-noted tendency to use Darwinian metaphors to describe individuals trapped by their background and circumstances into imprisoning patterns of belief and action. So in Lily Bart, Wharton tells us in a characteristic aside, "[i]nherited tendencies had combined with early training to make her the highly specialized product she was: an organism as helpless out of its narrow range as the sea-anemone torn from the rock."[4] Less immediately evident but more relevant to the issue of Wharton's attitude toward Jews is her willingness to rely heavily on race as a valid source for the characterization of individuals, a device that of course was extremely attractive to the patrician frame of mind.[5] The late nineteenth-century idea of race, as I have noted earlier in connection with Norris's Anglo-Saxonism, is intimately connected with evolutionary belief in that both Darwin and his popularizers held that races were distinctive biological entities that had evolved in a manner similar to that of species.[6] Races were like species in that some contained qualities that had permitted them to advance more swiftly than other races and in that they were incapable of successful mixing. In accord with this kind of thinking, a "foreign" race entering the territory of another race was in direct competition with the "native" race for the culture of that society because competition between races for dominance was inevitable and because assimilation of one race by the other was neither desirable or achievable. As I shortly discuss more fully, Wharton accepts fully this conception of race. Rosedale is not merely an Outsider who wishes entrée to the small, closed world of the New York elite, as might a nouveau riche Westerner; he is also the Jew who embodies within his nature a number of threatening and undesirable characteristics that are openly attributed to him by Wharton as characteristics of his race. As with Norris, Wharton had been able to draw upon a specific aspect of the new evolutionary thinking to bolster the ancient instinctive resentment against the Outsider in any form.

Before turning to *The House of Mirth,* it would be helpful to briefly discuss two works in which Wharton's tendency to negatively stereotype Jews appears in more conventional form than in that novel. My point in doing so is not to suggest that she is engaged in a similar, though more sophisticated, kind of effort in *The House of Mirth,* but rather to make clear that her portrait of Rosedale in *House,* while anti-Semitic in both tone and substance, is sufficiently nuanced to transcend any easy labeling.

"The Pot-Boiler," a short story involving young New York garret artists, appeared in December 1904, while Wharton was writing *The House of Mirth.* Its protagonist, Stanwell, initially declines to exploit his ability to turn out highly paid popular portraits in favor of pursuing his own artistic interests, but in the end does so in order to help a sick fellow artist and also to win the favor of the artist's sister. A Jew functions, as he often does in Wharton's and Cather's fiction dealing with artists, as the agent who facilitates Stanwell's prostitution of his talent. Shepson, a dealer, thus bears a rough similarity to the Jewish bankers who occupy demonized roles in Populist mythology in that he, too, is a middleman who profits from parasitically manipulating goods produced by others. He is not dishonest or underhanded; he merely provides a service within a culture that accepts the principle that financial success overrides all other values. And because the stereotype of the Jew stresses the centrality of the "commercial" in his life and values, who better than a Jew to represent the corrupting power of money in stories in which the theme is the conflict between an art of personal integrity and that of commercial success.

Wharton's three minor Jewish characters in *The Custom of the Country* (1913) derive from another anti-Semitic stereotype, that of the Jew as a social hanger-on, a figure who exploits, often nefariously, his partial acceptance into society for his own material well-being. It should be clear, however, that the novel as a whole is written in what can be called Wharton's extravagant satiric style, in which the device of the overdrawn caricature plays a major role. Although Wharton's portraits of the phony "Count" Aaronson, the sexually tainted Baroness Adelschein, and the over-suave art dealer Fleischhauer are grossly racist, this blatancy is not inappropriate to the novel's fictional method. The role of the three at the various points in which they appear is to express, each in his or her way, the devices that are required for Outsiders to reach even the periphery of the society they wish to enter. If one wants to scale the walled fortress that is Society, subterfuge is a necessary skill. The Austrian count is really a Jew from Cracow, the baroness negotiates sex for social acceptance, and the art dealer is ready to nail down a profitable deal for artworks behind the back of the French noble family owning them. A broad comic but racist theme characterizes the relationship of the novel's protagonist, Undine Spragg, to these caricatured portraits. The entire novel rests on the efforts of Undine, the daughter of a newly rich midwestern family, to enter New York and international society. She is at last, after many setbacks, successful in this attempt, having acquired in the course of the novel, in part through her relationships with the count, baroness, and art dealer, the techniques of phoniness, sexual rapaciousness, and outright dishonesty that are necessary to achieve this aim. She has, in a sense, learned that it is necessary to be a Jew if one is seeking a Jewish-like goal.

Unlike the Jews who are minor players in the various other Wharton novels and stories in which they appear, Simon Rosedale in *The House of Mirth* occupies center stage, second only to the protagonists Lily Bart and Lawrence Selden.[7] Indeed, he and Lily are engaged in the course of the novel in a thematic dynamic similar to that of Carrie and Hurstwood in Dreiser's *Sister Carrie,* though with reversed gender roles. Like Carrie, Rosedale at the opening of the work is outside the walled gate of the social world that he wishes to enter, but is on the edge of admission at its close; Lily, like Hurstwood, is initially within the walls and is an outcast at its conclusion. Carrie is handicapped in her struggle in that she is a penniless, untrained young woman from the provinces; Rosedale, although rich and financially astute, is even more severely handicapped by the fact that he is a Jew in turn-of-the-century New York.

Given his importance in the novel as a counterbalance to Lily, and given as well the importance of his Jewishness in that role, it is not surprising that Wharton introduces Rosedale at some length on his first appearance, when Lily meets him accidentally outside Selden's New York apartment. Rosedale is clearly an assimilated Germanic Jew. Blond and speaking unaccented if occasionally unpolished English, he also has an Anglicized name—perhaps Rosenfeld in the original. (It has been suggested that his name and social aspirations may allude to the banker August Belmont; the Belmonts, who had been Alsatian Jews, changed their original name, Schoenberg, to its French equivalent before immigrating to America.) But Rosedale is still in Wharton's mind above all the Jew, since she is at great pains to attribute his attitude and behavior to what she openly designates as his "race" or "blood." The first two such occasions occur during the novel's opening scene outside Selden's flat; two others occur later in the work. It would be useful to examine these four specific references to the biological source of Rosedale's character as a means of getting closer to Wharton's notion of the "Jewish race."

In the first such instance, Rosedale has already been described as possessing "small sidelong eyes which gave him the air of appraising people as if they were bric-a-brac" (14). Wharton then specifically attributes this quality to Rosedale's Jewishness when, in connection with his realization of Lily's social value to him if she appears with him in public, she notes that "[h]e had his race's accuracy in the appraisal of values, and to be seen walking down the platform at the crowded afternoon hour in the company of Miss Lily Bart would have been money in his pocket, as he might himself have phrased it" (15). Rosedale, we are also told during this opening scene, had gravitated toward Lily from their first meeting because, "with that mixture of artistic sensibility and business astuteness which characterizes his race" (16), he had realized from the first that she might be useful in the fulfillment of his social ambitions. The third such instance occurs later in the novel, when Rosedale has made a Wall Street killing and plans a huge mansion and impressive art collection to advance his social position. But, Wharton tells us, "[h]e knew he should have to go slowly, and the instincts of his race fitted him to suffer rebuffs and put up with delays" (121). The last such racial reference comes after Rosedale has proposed to Lily soon after the Tableau Vivant evening where she has made such a striking impression. He has couched the proposal in business terms as a good deal for the two of them. He has the wealth to lavish on a wife of social standing who would know how to achieve the grand style, and Lily, relatively poor but still socially acceptable, fits that role and would also glory in the playing of it. Lily, who is expecting Selden to arrive and to at last announce his feelings for her, does not dismiss him outright but rather postpones announcing her response, and Rosedale, "disciplined by the tradition of his blood to accept what was conceded" (178), agrees to wait for her final decision.

To Wharton, it would seem, to be Jewish means above all to possess an instinctive tendency toward commercial modes of belief and behavior, whatever the social context. (Rosedale is "Jewish" in other stereotypical ways—his "pushiness," for example, and his excessive interest in other people's affairs—but these, unlike those I cite above, are never directly attributed to him by Wharton as "racial" in origin.) Rosedale is not a Hester Street peddler shrewdly and even dishonestly hawking his wares, but he nevertheless brings to one of the most significant transactions of one's personal life, the choosing of a wife, something of the same frame of mind. He finds Lily attractive and also likes her; no doubt her beauty and histrionic flair (she is always "performing," Selden comments at one point), as revealed above all at the Tableau Vivant, have stimulated the artistic sensibility that Wharton also credits the Jewish temperament. But from the beginning to the end of the novel, his relations with her are above all shaped and controlled by her market value: he appears to be always weighing to what degree her current standing in the social world will aid or hinder him in his own effort to enter that world. Thus, the appropriateness, within the device of characterization by means of racial origins, of Rosedale's initial "appraisal" images in connection with Lily's market value followed by references to his policies of buyer caution and of accepting what is offered as he seeks to complete a purchase.

There is a vigorous debate among Wharton critics as to the degree of anti-Semitism reflected in her portrayal of Rosedale. Elizabeth Ammons is probably the most outspoken of those who fully condemn the characterization. To her, "[t]he book is about the snow-white heroine, the flower of Anglo-Saxon womanhood, not ending up married to the invading Jew."[8] Many critics, however, note that both Wharton and Lily appear to find Rosedale more and more acceptable as Lily's prospective husband as the novel progresses.[9] In striking contrast to Gus Trenor, who views Lily's need for money as an opportunity to prey upon her sexually, Rosedale's attitude and behavior are protective and kindly. He may be vulgar and pushy, Wharton appears to be saying, but (unlike Selden) he speaks his mind honestly, is kindhearted, and would—if he was not Jewish—make a suitable husband. In this interpretation of Rosedale, Wharton is held to be using his role as the wealthy Jewish outsider largely to highlight and satirize the limitations of those on the inside. Both insider and outsider are involved in a kind of game called "Society" in which it is presumed that background, family, and culture are required to play, but in which entrée is in fact based almost entirely, except for Jews, on wealth. A Jew such as Rosedale, who challenges this assumption openly by using his wealth to force his way into the game, reveals the hypocrisy at its core.

This is an appealing reading because, as is sometimes pointed out, Rosedale is the one likeable character in the novel. (Lily is its tragic protagonist, but she is not likable, and many readers, especially feminists, detest Selden.) He is similar to a Dickens character—he is always turning up with the same purpose in mind, in his case a desire to persuade Lily to marry him, a purpose that he pursues with a certain rough wit and charm. But to Wharton, although Rosedale may be a better man than those who despise him, he nevertheless, at the deepest level of his being, is still above all the Jew, in Wharton's sense of the less-than-admirable commercial instincts of the race.

This theme is revealed in Lily's final two meetings with Rosedale. In the first, in response to her telling him that she is now at last willing to marry him, he replies that, in effect, her market value has declined to the level where she is no longer a desirable commodity. Because enemies have spread rumors about her and she is no longer welcome in many homes, she can no longer play the role he had planned for her even though, he tells her, he loves her more than ever. To Lily, his announcement "made her feel herself no more than some superfine human merchandise" (256). Rosedale and Lily meet for a final time not long before her death, when she is in despair over her condition. She has rejected his earlier suggestion that she could legitimately blackmail her way back into social acceptance, and she has also used her last financial resource, her legacy, to repay Trenor his loans, a gesture that Rosedale admires as "fine" (293). As he and Lily leave the tearoom where they have been talking, Rosedale tosses a bill on the table and then "paused to make sure of his change" (293).

In the end, therefore, it is Lily who has the strength to rise above the incubus of birth that has haunted her throughout the novel. Loving money for the comforts and pleasures it has provided her since childhood, she is nevertheless capable of calling upon the ineluctable "fineness" in her nature to reject the suspect means necessary to preserve her position in her world. Rosedale, however, for all his love of and admiration for Lily, is too much the Jew to be able to rise to an analogous level of self-sacrifice in the name of either love or honor. Lily, as an item of merchandise in the marriage market, is now no longer of any value to him in that context, and he is a man who always acts in response to the market just as he always counts his change. He has survived, and will continue to advance toward his goals, Wharton implies, just as the Jew has always done—by dint of his "commercial" instincts.

Willa Cather, like Edith Wharton, wrote a number of short stories in which Jews play minor though significant roles, and one important and finely wrought novel, *The Professor's House* (1925), in which a Jew is featured prominently in the work's themes. Again like Wharton, Cather's response to the Jewish presence in American life rests on a foundation of patrician distrust of the supposed Jewish emphasis on the economic in all matters and a corresponding distaste for such attributes of the Jewish character as greed and coarseness held to derive from that emphasis. The two writers differ primarily in their thematic deployment of this suspicion of the Jew. Wharton, whose best work stems from a satiric vision of the limitations of her own class, often—as in the case of Rosedale—used the Jew to mirror these limitations; in Rosedale we see the emptiness of what he aspires to achieve and of what Lily fails to hold on to. Cather, however, although she too was a critic of early twentieth-century American life, sought to render this theme by comparing a past of spiritual strength and commitment to high ideals with a present lacking these values. Her basic vision of life was elegiac rather than satiric. The Jew, although he is rendered satirically in several of her short stories, thus appears in *The Professor's House* as a representative of those new elements in American life that fail to honor the richness of our past.

Like Hamlin Garland, Cather appears to have acquired a willingness to accept anti-Semitic stereotypes from her exposure to them during her early years on the western prairie during the height of the Populist movement. Although she spent the first ten years of her life in Virginia, she lived in Nebraska from 1883 to 1896, first on a farm, then in the small farming town of Red Cloud, and, finally, as a college student, in Lincoln. John H. Randall made a convincing case many years ago, in his *The Landscape and the Looking Glass,* for Cather's absorption during her late teens and early twenties of at least a portion of the Populist anti-Semitism of this area and period. As Randall points out, Cather's later theme of the loss in contemporary American culture of the strength and courage of the early prairie settlers is analogous to the Populist vision of the destruction of the independent farmer by international Jewish bankers.[10]

Like many of the writers of her period, Cather usually failed to accept the contradiction between the benevolence and culture of the few Jews she knew personally and her acceptance of popular racial stereotypes. Thus, on the one hand, she benefited greatly in her teens from a Red Cloud Jewish shopkeeping family, the Wieners, who introduced her to the German and French classics, a family she paid homage to in her late story "Old Mrs. Harris."[11] On the other hand, there is the remarkable sketch she wrote in November 1893 for the *Nebraskan State Journal,* when, at just under twenty, she was at the outset of her career in journalism. The sketch is about a baby and begins, "He is a peculiar-looking baby. He has the unmistakable chin and the unmistakable nose of an unmistakable race, . . . one of the oldest races in the world." As the baby lies in his carriage, "he looks as if he might be thinking over some old business transaction that he conducted . . . some three thousand years ago." He begins to cry, and his mother gives him a penny to play with. "He reaches out for it eagerly and looks at it carefully on both sides as though seeing if it were genuine. Then he folds his long thin little fingers over it, and settles back on his pillow with a long sigh of content, and dreams of the things he will sell when he is a man."[12] Although untitled, the sketch might well be titled "The Baby Shylock" or some such variation to indicate its deep roots in both the traditional myth and current Populist rhetoric, and is a remarkable anti-Semitic exercise in its own right. Of course, Cather's later portrayals of Jews are usually more complex, but in a sense all her Jewish characters, as we will see, are still clutching a penny in one form or another and dreaming of some form of material advancement.

Other than her late nineteenth-century prairie background, Cather's anti-Semitism, at least in its post-1916 manifestations, may also have a deeply personal source. I say "may" because there is no factual evidence that the 1916 marriage of her longtime close friend and companion Isabelle McClung to the Jewish musician Jan Hambourg contributed to the anti-Semitic tendency in her work, in particular to the portrayal of Louie Marcellus in *The Professor's House.* Rather, there are events in Cather's life and aspects of her writing that can lead one to speculate on a possible connection between the two, a connection that even Cather herself may not have been aware of.[13]

McClung and Cather met in 1899, in Pittsburgh.[14] They soon established a close relationship, though whether it was physically consummated is uncertain. It was apparently not exclusive, however, for in 1903 Cather established a similar relationship with Edith Lewis, and for the next thirteen years she lived principally with Lewis in New York but often traveled with McClung. After McClung's marriage to Hambourg, she and Cather continued to see a great deal of each other, as Cather lived with the Hambourgs in New Hampshire, Toronto, and near Paris for several extensive periods between 1916 and 1925. In short, there appears to have been an acceptance before McClung's marriage that Cather could be engaged in other relationships, and there was an acceptance after the marriage that the friendship could continue. Yet, as one commentator has it, Cather was "surprised and devastated" by the marriage,[15] and, as several critics have speculated, may have transferred her anger to Hambourg, whom she also did not care for personally, and thus into the portrayal of Louie Marcellus in *The Professor's House* as a cultivated but basically materialistic Jew who symbolizes his control of the conditions of modern life by marrying a Gentile woman. And even regarding Hambourg there is mixed evidence, since Cather after all did dedicate the novel to him, something that she must have done either tongue-in-cheek or in unawareness of the deepest sources of her characterization of Marcellus. All in all, it is perhaps safest to say that there is considerable evidence of Cather's antiSemitism before McClung's marriage[16] and that the evidence of the possible impact of the marriage on her fiction is ambiguous. The depiction of Marcellus may owe something to Cather's chagrin over "losing" McClung to a Jew, but his characterization can also be fully explained by previously present themes in Cather's work. McClung's marriage was therefore perhaps a catalyst for the expression of these themes in a major novel, but it was not itself their source.

Thus, two stories written long before the McClung-Hambourg marriage contain in rough form when considered jointly the basic anti-Semitic paradigm present in Cather's portrait of Marcellus. In "The Marriage of Phaedra," a story that appeared initially in Cather's 1905 collection *The Troll Garden*, Lichtenstein, an Austrian Jewish art dealer provided with a comic accent and of "repulsive personality and innate vulgarity,"[17] is instrumental in attempting to betray the heritage of the dead artist Treffinger by irresponsibly disposing of his great last work, "The Marriage of Phaedra." Resembling several of Wharton's crass Jewish enablers, Lichtenstein is foreign, uncouth, and a key player in the disposal of Treffinger's estate in a manner in which the monetary trumps all other values. Cather's "Behind the Singer Tower" of 1912 transfers these stereotypical Shylock characteristics to the more threatening figure of the thoroughly assimilated and cultivated Jew. Although Merryweather, an engineer, is only half-Jewish and is not Semitic in appearance, he still possesses, we are told, "racial characteristics."[18] These include a swiftness of mind, an aggressive personality, and a disregard for those standing in his way. "He didn't know there had ever been such a thing as modesty or reverence in the world" (48). As Marcellus will do, he uses his wife, with questionable taste, to display his success. "He married a burgeoning Jewish beauty, . . . and he hung her with the jewels of the East until she looked like the Song of Solomon done into motion pictures" (48). Most damning of all, he adopts dangerous cost-cutting measures in one of his enterprises that lead to the death of innocent workmen. Together, Lichtenstein and Merryweather constitute Cather's acceptance of the patrician interpretation of the threat posed by the Jewish presence in early twentieth-century American life. The uncouth first-generation Jew has been replaced by his assimilated and suave descendant, but both share similar undesirable racial characteristics, and the later example of the species is the more dangerous of the two.

Two of Cather's most well-known anti-Semitic stories, "The Diamond Mine" and "Scandal," are also of interest in that both appeared not long after McClung's marriage (the first in late 1916, the second in 1919), and both depict Jews preying on non-Jewish women artists—a theme that lends credence to the premise that Cather was deeply hurt by the marriage. In the first story, Cressida is a "diamond mine" in the sense that her great success as a diva has provided anyone associated with her with a good income. This includes above all her discoverer and agent, the Greek Jew Poppas. Poppas is very much in the Svengali mode of anti-Semitic caricature. (*Trilby* is actually mentioned in the story.) "He was a vulture of the vulture race," we are told, "and he had the beak of one."[19] It is characteristic of their relationship that when she dies on the *Titanic,* he was not traveling with her and is also awarded $50,000 by her will. In the second story, "Scandal," Stein is an Austrian Jewish immigrant who began in the New York garment trade and now is a millionaire department store owner. Wishing to advance in society but held to be "one of the most hideous men in New York,"[20] he victimizes well-known women, including the opera singer Kitty Ayrshire, by having other women resembling them accompany him to fashionable events. Though impostors, their presence nevertheless creates the rumor, advantageous to Stein's social aspirations, that he has succeeded in attracting well-known beauties. Stein later marries a Jewish heiress and acquires "a great house on Fifth Avenue that used to belong to people of a very different sort" (463). The story ends with Kitty telling of a party at the Stein home, filled with "women [who] glittered like Christmas-trees" and "Old Testament characters" (464–65), an occasion in which the atmosphere "was somehow so thick and personal." Kitty sums her sense of Stein and his world of flashy, rich, and unscrupulous Jews as the irreducibly alien in American life with the comment that "[t]hese people were all too—well, too much what they were" (466).

This tendency in Cather's as well as Wharton's fiction containing Jewish figures to allegorize a fear of the Jew seeking entrée into American social life into a portrait of the Jew as sexual predator, violating in one form or another Gentile women to gain this end, reaches a climax in Cather's story "The Old Beauty," written in 1936 but not published until 1948. The "old beauty" has just died and, in recounting her story, a former friend recalls a difficult moment in her life when despite her great beauty and social prominence, she is in financial difficulties and seeks aid from a New York banker. The banker, "a stout, dark man,"[21] is an immigrant Jew "who has made a lot of money" (720) but who "under his smoothness [is] a vulgar person" (716). During their discussion of his possible aid, the banker pins her against a couch and thrusts his hand down her bodice.

*The Professor's House* is a highly schematized work.[22] Almost every detail of landscape, social practice, and human interaction in the novel contributes to the fundamental opposition in the novel between a past culture in which one could pursue values outside of personal gain and a contemporary world in which efforts of this kind are impossible. It would be best, then, to begin with Tom Outland, a figure who is dead at the opening of the novel but whose life story, as we come to know it, dramatizes this lost Eden in which the human potential for grandeur of soul still existed.

Tom functions in several areas of the ideal as conceived by Cather. First, he is an American success story in that he had worked his way, by dint of strength of mind and will, from neglected orphan to research physicist. Also, with the exception of one fortuitous discovery, he has devoted himself to "pure" research. Most of all, he responded instinctively to the complex beauty of the ancient Indian civilization he discovered in New Mexico and had worked hard to ensure the preservation of its remaining ruins and artifacts. And finally, with the onset of the European war, he had died as a volunteer in the French Foreign Legion. Embodied in these various activities is a mind-set that Cather deeply admires—the capacity to absorb from the land (New Mexico in this case) and from those who worked it a desire both to preserve the traditions and values derived from that interaction of land and people and to translate these traditions and values into a living code for the present. This, as Cather makes clear in the novel's long inset tale "Tom Outland's Story," which deals with his experience in New Mexico before his later life as a physicist, is not a conscious process but rather arises out of some mysterious human capacity to derive transcendent meanings from material experience. All such efforts to transcend the material, Cather implies, are inherently tragic. The pure and high civilization Tom discovered, one that "lived for something more than food and shelter,"[23] was destroyed by more primitive war tribes, and Tom's efforts to preserve the remnants of that civilization were stymied by his money-hungry friend Roddy and by Washington bureaucrats. Nevertheless, although Tom's story was tragic in several senses, it was also heroic and inspiring. People could at that time, as Tom had done, seek to act out the noble and pure strains potential in human nature.

Professor St. Peter is the link between Tom's values and ways of life and those of the present. A scholar of Spanish adventurers in North America, he has worked long and hard on his opus under difficult conditions and is now attempting to bring its final volumes to completion. St. Peter aided Tom when he arrived many years earlier at the university as a penniless student, and it was perhaps inevitable that Tom and St. Peter's daughter Rosamond would later become engaged. But now—in the principal theme of the portion of the novel set in the present—St. Peter feels himself besieged by the materialistic demands of contemporary life and inadequate to maintain the values of his "son" Tom. He senses that he is fighting losing battles both in warding off the increasing commercialization of academic life and the expensive lifestyle cultivated by his wife and Rosamond. Much of this pressure on St. Peter is symbolized by dwellings. Lillian, his wife, had persuaded him to build a larger and more impressive house to replace the old, uncomfortable home where they had raised their children and where he had done all his writing, and Rosamond and her husband Marcellus are building a grand mansion near Lake Michigan. In retreat from this world, St. Peter spends more and more time brooding about the past in general and Tom in particular in the study of his otherwise deserted old house.

Louie Marcellus embodies in one figure all that St. Peter finds lacking in a world that no longer contains Tom Outlands to counter its crass commercialism. Not that Louie is himself a traditional immigrant Shylock figure; like Rosedale, he is a thoroughly assimilated Jew—only recognizably Jewish in his nose, we are told—and generous, playful, and cultured. Nevertheless, to

St. Peter he is in several senses a usurper, one who in the act of seizure has corrupted that which he now possesses. Most obviously, he had taken over both Rosamond, who was Tom's fiancée, and Tom's patent. An engineer by training, he has through entrepreneurial skill made a fortune commercially exploiting Tom's discovery, and he has through his generosity, insofar as Rosamond and her mother are concerned, developed in them a taste for the expensive and grand.

St. Peter feels himself threatened by Marcellus—not merely by the temptation of wealth but by wealth in the hand of a Jew. Marcellus, to St. Peter, is too much the ingratiating Jew who is too anxious to please. He is too generous, too eager to push his enthusiasms upon others, and too showy—all of which constitute to St. Peter a "florid style" (125). Mrs. St. Peter tries, perhaps facetiously and certainly unsuccessfully, to excuse Marcellus's disregard of conventional decorum by pointing out that "the Oriental peoples didn't have an Age of Chivalry" (125), an allusion to the widespread anti-Semitic belief that the Jewish race was in part Asian in origin. To St. Peter, however, Louie represents not only the commercial spirit of the age alien to the spirit of a Tom Outland but also the outsider who is "alien" in his behavior. Because all is now money and show, St. Peter appears to surmise, who best to express those qualities in one figure than a Jew.

The subtle appeal of Cather's narrative stems in part from its lack of excess. Louie is a good man who wishes to do no one harm, and the money provided by Tom's invention has brought a more comfortable life to both families. Yet St. Peter broods and is unhappy and comes close to death in his old study in an accident that has a suicidal component. It is characteristic of a culture, Cather appears to be saying, to make itself palatable and even desirable, whatever its underlying flaws, to all but the most discriminating spirit. For the culture of early twentieth-century America, life is too pleasant with one's comfortable home, new possessions, and long holidays to sense what has been lost, and there are no longer nefarious Shylock-like Jewish bankers to dramatize the evil of the forces in power but rather a cultivated and kind Louie Marcellus. So even St. Peter, after his near-death accident, decides to accept rather than bemoan his condition, and Marcellus the Jew remains in control of what had been Tom's and the professor's world.

# Epilogue

Anti-Semitism was a pervasive element in the thinking of many of the new writers who emerged during the 1890s. Although the prejudice never reached the virulence found in a Dostoevsky or Celine, it was nevertheless a distinct presence. For Hamlin Garland, anti-Semitism was largely a closet belief, expressed principally in his diaries and later autobiographies. For the other writers I have discussed, however, it found its way into their fiction, often in relation to significant strands of plot and theme. Although all the writers I include in this study had Jewish friends and acquaintances, a few—notably Theodore Dreiser and Willa Cather—derived at least some of their bias from difficult personal and business relationships with specific Jews.

Despite this understandable diversity in their personal experience of Jews and in the forms used to express their belief, the anti-Semitism of these writers share a number of common elements. All were responding in varying degrees both to significant social events of their time and to currents of belief that had arisen in response to these events. Chief among these were the western farm depression and consequent Populist revolt of the 1880s and 1890s and the onset of the great immigration to America of eastern European Jews in the 1880s, both of which encouraged the acceptance of economic and racial theorizing prejudicial toward Jews. Norris's figures of Zerkow in *McTeague* and S. Behrman in *The Octopus,* for example, offer clear instances of the ancient Shylock image infused with elements drawn from events and ideas of Norris's own time and place. Other writers are more indirect, but all reflect in varying degrees beliefs derived from a contemporary ethos that denigrated the Jewish presence in America.

The anti-Semitism in the writers I have been discussing is of course a phase in the long and often bitter history of American nativist belief. Almost from the founding of the country to the present, Americans who were themselves descendants of immigrants have attacked as undesirable each fresh wave of newcomers. The writers who came to maturity in the 1890s, however, express as well in their anti-Semitism two additional blind spots in self-perception. These writers considered themselves in one form or another as "advanced" in their thinking. Whether it was a participation in left-wing politics (Dreiser), a desire to improve western farm conditions (Garland), attacks on monopolistic business practices (Norris), or sympathetic portrayals of women seeking to break down barriers against individual fulfillment (Wharton and Cather), they tended to view themselves as seeking to express in their writing a greater need in America for social justice and personal freedom. Yet they failed to perceive a relationship between this frame of mind and the average Jew seeking the same justice and freedom in the face of immense hurdles and handicaps. An almost surreal instance of this blindness can be found in the thinking of Jack London, who viewed Socialism as a paradise of social equality to come but who refused to consider Jews, because they were of "degenerate" stock, as potential participants in this Eden.[1]

A second failure of self-perception is closely related to the first. Deeply influenced by Darwinian belief, writers of this generation frequently portrayed characters whose lives and beliefs are shaped and often controlled by the social reality and ideas of their time and place. For example, Dreiser's and Wharton's nuanced portrayals of this kind of environmental determinism in *An American Tragedy* and *The Age of Innocence,* portraits that involve the imprisoning impact of contemporary custom and belief on a character's thinking, are among the glories of their fiction. And yet all of these writers failed to recognize that their own ideas about Jews were deeply "environmental" in their source—that these beliefs were as much a condition of their moment as those ideas about America's supposed social equality and the inferiority of women that they were attacking in their novels.

# Notes

## Introduction

1. From Garland's draft of a letter to John Spargo, 20 December 1920, in the Hamlin Garland Collection, Doheny Library, University of Southern California, Los Angeles. I wish to thank Keith Newlin for bringing this correspondence to my attention.

2. See the discussion of Garland and Ford in chapter 1.

3. See, for example, Poliakov, *History of Anti-Semitism*, 3: 41–46, and Lindemann, *Esau's Tears*, 251–61.

4. There is no general study of the American literary anti-Semitism of this period, though Harap includes brief comments on this strain in his *Image of the Jew in American Literature* and *Creative Awakening*.

5. Milosz, *Native Realm*, 94.

6. For general discussions of late nineteenth- and early twentieth-century American anti-Semitism, see Higham, *Send These to Me*; Dobkowski, *Tarnished Dream*; Gerber, "Anti-Semitism and Jewish-Gentile Relations," in Gerber, *Anti-Semitism in American History*; Cohen, "Antisemitism in the Gilded Age," in Gurock, *Anti-Semitism in America*; and Singerman, "The Jew as Racial Alien," in Gerber, *Anti-Semitism in American History*.

7. The most well-known discussion of Populist anti-Semitism is by Hofstadter in his *Age of Reform*, 77–81. Among other accounts, see Higham, *Send These to Me*, and Cohen, "Antisemitism in the Gilded Age."

8. See Dinnerstein, *Antisemitism in America*, 50.

9. For the history of this migration, see Diner, *Jews of the United States*, and Sorin, *Time for Building*.

10. Brief accounts of the patrician element in late nineteenth-century American anti-Semitism can be found in Higham's *Send These to Me*, 130–31, and his *Strangers in the Land*, 138–44.

11. The standard work in this area is Gossett, *Race: The History of an Idea in America*; I have also profited from Robert Singerman's important essay "The Jew as Racial Alien."

12. For the "Long March" theme in late nineteenth-century American historiography, in addition to Gossett's chapter on Anglo-Saxonism in his *Race,* see Jones, "Arms of the Anglo-Saxons," in *The Theory of American Literature*; Saveth, "Race and Nationalism in American Historiography"; and Higham, *Strangers in the Land,* 133–39, 165–75.

## Chapter 1: Hamlin Garland

1. It is no doubt for this reason that histories of American anti-Semitism seldom contain discussions of Garland. Perhaps the fullest account occurs in Harap's *Image of the Jew in American Literature,* 389–91.

2. In the account of Garland's political beliefs and activities during 1887–92 that follows, I draw upon two of my works: "Hamlin Garland in the *Standard*" and *Hamlin Garland's Early Work.*

3. See Hicks, *Populist Revolt,* 443.

4. *Standard,* 3 February 1892, 7–8; reprinted in Pizer, *Hamlin Garland's Early Work,* 93–94.

5. Garland's movements during the early 1890s are difficult to chart with full accuracy, since, as he recounts in *Son of the Middle Border,* he "travelled almost incessantly for nearly two years" (424) and kept no record of his journeys. Reports of his activities by the *Standard* and other newspapers, however, confirm these two extended trips.

6. Hofstadter, *Age of Reform,* 77–81. For an extended reply to Hofstadter, see Nugent, *Tolerant Populists.* Many of the essays collected by Gerber and Gurock allude to the controversy; see Gerber, *Anti-Semitism in American History*; Gurock, *Anti-Semitism in America.*

7. Harvey, *Coin's Financial School,* 215.

8. For Bryan's Cross of Gold speech and anti-Semitism, see Dinnerstein, *Antisemitism in America,* 49–50.

9. The only book-length study of Lease, Richard Stiller's *Queen of Populists: The Story of Mary Elizabeth Lease* (New York: Crowell, 1970), is intended for teenage readers. In addition to the entry in volume 13 of the *American National Biography* (1999), see Diggs, "Women in the Alliance Movement," and Nugent, *Tolerant Populists,* 80–84. *A Spoil of Office* was published by the Arena Publishing Company of Boston in September 1892 after appearing serially in the *Arena* magazine earlier that year. It was reprinted in 1969 in a facsimile edition by Johnson Reprint Company.

10. Garland, *Roadside Meetings,* 187, 186. The fullest and best discussion of the political background of *A Spoil of Office* is Martin's "'This Spreading Radicalism.'" Martin, however, only mentions in passing that Lease served as the model for Ida Wilbur (43).

11. See the frontispiece photograph in Diggs, "Women in the Alliance Movement."

12. Garland, *Son of the Middle Border,* 421.

13. See the *Los Angeles Times,* 4 July 1892, for a report of the occasion.

14. Garland, *Son of the Middle Border,* 423.

15. See Nixon, "Populist Movement in Iowa," 59.

16. Nugent, *Tolerant Populists,* 83.

17. Cohen, "Antisemitism in the Gilded Age," in Gurock, *Anti-Semitism in America,* 274.

18. Lease, *Problem of Civilization Solved,* 319–20.

19. Garland, *Crumbling Idols,* 176–77.

20. For Zangwill, the Guggenheims, Kahn, and the Lewisohns, see Pizer, ed., *Hamlin Garland's Diaries,* 199–200, 141, 162, 164; for Guiterman, see Garland, *Afternoon Neighbors,* 112. References to *Hamlin Garland's Diaries* and to *Afternoon Neighbors* will hereafter appear in the text.

21. Garland, *My Friendly Contemporaries,* 206–7.

22. Garland, *Back-Trailers from the Middle Border,* 81.

23. For Ford's anti-Semitism, I have relied principally on Lee, *Henry Ford and the Jews*; Ribuffo, "Henry Ford and *The International Jew*," in Gurock, *Anti-Semitism in America*; and Baldwin, *Henry Ford and the Jews.*

24. Lee, *Henry Ford and the Jews,* 14.

25. Garland wrote Fred L. Black, the *Independent*'s business manager, on 20 December 1926, noting that he had prepared an article about his recent meeting with Ford and asking if Black could review it and also gain Ford's permission to publish before Garland submitted it to "one of the big magazines." He concluded: "In 'Jew York' Ford is a bogey man, a wild man. I would like to make record of that side of him which it was my privilege to see." See Newlin and McCullough, eds., *Selected Letters of Hamlin Garland,* 332.

26. Ford and Garland also shared an enthusiasm for the McGuffey Readers, a series of school texts widely used during the late nineteenth century to introduce children to literature (see Baldwin, *Henry Ford and the Jews,* 5, and Garland, *Son of the Middle Border,* 112). Baldwin points out, in his *Henry Ford and the Jews,* 2–6, that the readers are permeated with material containing anti-Semitic passages.

27. Higham, *Send These to Me,* 187–88.

## Chapter 2: Frank Norris

1. Norris, "Case for Lombroso," reprinted in McElrath and Burgess, eds., *Apprenticeship Writings of Frank Norris,* vol. 2. Citations of the story in the text are from *Apprenticeship Writings.*

2. As Higham points out in his *Strangers in the Land,* 140, the popular conception of the Anglo-Saxon strain in America, a conception shared by Norris, was that

the strain included not only descendants of the Germanic tribes that had invaded England but all northern Europeans as well.

3. The magazine at one time was subtitled "A Journal for Those in the Swim." See McElrath and Crisler, *Frank Norris*, 200.

4. See Starr, *Americans and the California Dream,* and Almaguer, *Racial Fault Lines.*

5. See *McTeague,* where Marcus exclaims, "Ah, the Chinese cigar-makers. . . . It's them as is ruining the cause of white labor" (72).

6. See, for example, Norris's accounts of the Portuguese and Mexicans engaged in the rabbit hunt in book 2, chapter 6, of *The Octopus* and of the Chinese pirates in *Moran of the Lady Letty.*

7. I discuss Lombroso's beliefs and their influence on Norris's portrayal of Mc-Teague in my *Novels of Frank Norris,* 56–63.

8. The clipping is in the Frank Norris Collection, Bancroft Library, University of California, Berkeley.

9. Nordau, *Degeneration,* 17. Further citations will appear in the text.

10. Information about Norris's University of California course work is gathered from records at the Registrar's Office, University of California, Berkeley, and from Franklin Walker's comments on this material in the Franklin Walker Collection, Bancroft Library, University of California, Berkeley.

11. Pizer, *Novels of Frank Norris,* 12–22.

12. Le Conte, *Evolution,* 375 (Le Conte's emphasis).

13. San Francisco *Wave* 16 (4 September 1897): 2. This unsigned editorial was attributed to Norris by his initial biographer, Franklin Walker, as well by several other Norris scholars. Although the eminent Norris scholar Joseph R. McElrath, Jr., questions the attribution in his *Frank Norris and "The Wave,"* I have chosen to accept Walker's attribution because both the language and themes of the editorial strongly resemble Norris's other writing on the subject. For one of Norris's fullest later endorsements of the Long March idea, see "The Frontier Gone at Last" (February 1902), reprinted in Pizer, ed., *Literary Criticism of Frank Norris.*

14. Le Conte, "Race Problem in the South," in *Man and the State,* 359, 360. Further citations will appear in the text. See also Haller's discussion of Le Conte's racism in his *Outcasts from Evolution,* 154–66.

15. Gayley, "English at the University of California," 31. See also Kurtz, *Charles Mills Gayley,* 34.

16. See Pizer, *Novels of Frank Norris,* 11, 182n16.

17. See Kahn, *Science and Aesthetic Judgment.*

18. Gayley's popular *The Classic Myths in English Literature* (1893) included a section on Germanic and Norse myths.

19. Crane and Moses, *Politics,* 70–71.

20. Moses, "Data of Mexican and United States History," 29–30. It is of interest that Moses was appointed by President McKinley in 1900 to the Philippine Commission, the agency that administered the islands following their occupation by U.S. forces.

21. *Vandover and the Brute,* in Norris, ed. Pizer, *Novels and Essays,* 91. Further citations will appear in the text.

22. Harap, *Image of the Jew in American Literature,* 391; Levine, *Merchant of Modernism,* 70.

23. Norris, *McTeague,* 28. Further citations will appear in the text.

24. The phrase is from Pick, *Svengali's Web,* 136.

25. For Svengali and *Trilby,* see Pick, *Svengali's Web,* and Dijkstra, *Idols of Perversity,* 34–36.

26. See McElrath and Crisler, *Frank Norris,* 132–33.

27. In addition to "A Case for Lombroso," see in particular Norris's early stories "Outward and Visible Signs. V. Thoroughbred" (*Overland Monthly,* February 1895) and "A Defense of the Flag" (*Argonaut,* 28 October 1895). In these stories, Shotover, a San Francisco thoroughbred, behaves heroically when confronted by Irish thugs and Chinese coolies.

28. Forrey, in "The 'Jew' in Norris' *The Octopus,*" 202–3, notes that he was unable to identify a Jew employed by the Southern Pacific who played a role similar to Behrman's in the Mussel Slough incident. Forrey also notes, however, that a Jew did serve as an agent of the railroad in a shady San Joaquin land deal some ten years prior to Mussel Slough.

29. Richard Chase and Kenneth S. Lynn made this identification in the 1950s; see Chase, *American Novel and Its Tradition,* 195, and Lynn, *Dream of Success,* 191. Harap's comment appears in his *Creative Awakening,* 27. For Forrey, see "The 'Jew' in Norris' *The Octopus.*"

30. *The Octopus,* in Norris, ed. Pizer, *Novels and Essays,* 629. Further citations will appear in the text.

31. Harvey, *Coin's Financial School,* 215.

32. It is worth noting that the novel contains an explicit paean to Anglo-Saxon virtues in Norris's description of the picnic following a rabbit drive: "It was Homeric, this feasting, this vast consuming of meat and bread and wine, followed now by games of strength. An epic simplicity and directness, an honest Anglo-Saxon mirth and innocence, commended it. Crude it was; coarse it was, but no taint of viciousness was here. These people were good people, kindly, benignant even, always readier to give than to receive. They were good stock. Of such was the backbone of the nation— sturdy Americans everyone of them. Where else in the world round were such strong, honest men, such strong, beautiful women?" (979–80).

## Chapter 3: Theodore Dreiser

1. Many commentators have mentioned Dreiser's anti-Semitism in passing. Perhaps the fullest accounts are by Tuerk, "*American Spectator* Symposium Controversy," and Harap, "Theodore Dreiser," in *Creative Awakening,* 128–42. Tuerk's study is limited to the mid-1930s.

2. Dreiser, *Dawn,* 558. Further citations will appear in the text.

3. The passage has a complicated compositional history, one that bears on the distinction within it between Dreiser's account of his 1891 attitude toward Jews and his later qualification of this attitude. The holograph version of the passage (at the Lilly Library, Indiana University) contains neither the concluding sentence about "the possible beauty of the individual soul" nor the phrases "race prejudice, possibly" and "as I then pictured them to myself." Both the sentence and the phrases are in the typescript of *Dawn* in Box 243, the Dreiser Papers, University of Pennsylvania Library (hereafter indicated as Dreiser Papers). Dreiser wrote *Dawn* during 1914–17 and initially revised it in late 1917, when he had Louise Campbell prepare a typescript of the entire holograph. He wrote to Campbell on 20 October 1917 (see Dreiser, *Letters to Louise*, 13) that "I want first a single rough copy which I can correct, and then I want an original and a carbon of the corrected copy," a procedure that may explain why the added material does not appear in the holograph but is in typed form in the typescript; that is, Dreiser added it by hand on the now-missing "rough copy" of the typescript, from where it was copied into the extant corrected typescript. Dreiser's letter to George L. Wheelock on 17 November 1920 (Elias, ed., *Letters of Theodore Dreiser*, 1: 301), in which he reports that *Dawn* was typed and "ready," suggests that the entire revision was completed by that date at the latest. Dreiser then further revised the book in 1930, again with Campbell's aid, in preparation for its 1931 publication by Horace Liveright. These various strands of evidence suggest that in reviewing the initial typescript of *Dawn* in 1917–18, Dreiser realized that the original passage did not reflect his current ideas about Jews and revised it accordingly. (I am indebted to Stephen Brennan for aid in consulting the *Dawn* manuscripts that I refer to.)

4. The best account of the history of the play, from original idea to publication and production, is by Newlin and Rusch in their edition of *The Collected Plays of Theodore Dreiser*, xx–xxxiii, 340–47.

5. Liptzin, *Jew in American Literature*, 159. For a similar view, see Schiff, "Shylock's Mishpocheh," in Gerber, ed., *Anti-Semitism in American History*, 88.

6. Cahan to Dreiser, 14 December 1921 (Dreiser Papers), and Dreiser to Cahan, 23 December 1921, in Pizer, ed., *Theodore Dreiser: A Picture and a Criticism of Life*, 95.

7. Dreiser to A. Heller, 25 May 1938, in Pizer, ed., *Theodore Dreiser: A Picture and a Criticism of Life*: "If anyone thinks that basically I am anti-semitic he or she should read *The Hand of the Potter*" (241).

8. Dreiser to A. Heller, 25 May 1938, in Pizer, ed., *Theodore Dreiser: A Picture and a Criticism of Life*, 241; Dreiser also made this claim in a number of other letters of this period.

9. Cahan, "Unusual Jewish Tragedy in an Unusual Theater," 4. I am indebted to Fannie Yoker for a translation of the review from the Yiddish.

10. Newlin and Rusch discuss this source fully in *Collected Plays;* see note 4 above.

11. Newlin and Rusch, eds., *Collected Plays*, 263.

12. Dreiser to Mencken, 5 November 1922, in Riggio, ed., *Dreiser-Mencken Letters,* 2: 481. Dreiser's comment was known as early as 1959, however, when it appeared in Elias, ed., *Letters of Theodore Dreiser,* 2: 405.

13. Swanberg, *Dreiser,* 267.

14. Dreiser, *The Titan,* 202, 476.

15. Dreiser, *An American Tragedy,* Riggio, ed., 116.

16. J[ean] J[affe], "Dreiser Wants to Know More About Us," *The Day* (New York), 13 April 1924, n. p. Reprinted in Rusch and Pizer, eds., *Theodore Dreiser: Interviews,* 95–97.

17. Berenice C. Skidelsky, "America and Her Jews," *Jewish Advocate* (Boston), 5 February 1920, p. 7, and "'As Yeast Added to the Nation's Making': Theodore Dreiser, North American Novelist, Gives His Impression of the Jews," *New York Jewish News,* 12 February 1920. Reprinted in Rusch and Pizer, eds., *Theodore Dreiser: Interviews,* 69–70.

18. A similar emphasis on the contribution of immigrant Jews to the spectacle of New York life occurs in Dreiser's sketch "The City Awakes," in *The Color of a Great City,* when he comments on their "adding rich, dark, colorful threads to the rug or tapestry which is New York" (6).

19. See Singerman, "The Jew as Racial Alien: The Genetic Component of American Anti-Semitism," in Gerber, ed., *Anti-Semitism in American History,* 103–28.

20. Both Swanberg, *Dreiser,* 306, and Dardis, *Fireband,* 201, note Dreiser's belief that Lasky and Liveright had conspired in advance of the meeting to keep the price low.

21. Dreiser to Kiendl, 18 August 1930, in Pizer, ed., *Theodore Dreiser: A Picture and a Criticism of Life,* 144–45.

22. Sulamith Ish-Kishor, "Dreiser Looks at the Russian Jews," *The Day* (New York), 10 February 1929, p. 1. Reprinted in Rusch and Pizer, eds., *Theodore Dreiser: Interviews,* 171–75.

23. Raymond Dannenbaum, "Theodore Dreiser Discounts Intermarriage," *Jewish Journal* (San Francisco) 3 (4 June 1930): 3, 16. Reprinted in Rusch and Pizer, eds., *Theodore Dreiser: Interviews,* 208–14.

24. See Victor C. Ferkiss, "Populist Influences on American Fascism," *Western Political Quarterly* (1957), in Gurock, ed., *Anti-Semitism in America,* 301–24, and Ribuffo, "Henry Ford and *The International Jew,*" in Gurock, ed., *Anti-Semitism in America,* 413–53.

25. See Synnott, "Anti-Semitism and American Universities: Did Quotas Follow the Jews?" in Gerber, ed., *Anti-Semitism in American History,* 233–71.

26. Dreiser to Anderson, 12 May 1933, in Pizer, ed., *Theodore Dreiser: A Picture and a Criticism of Life,* 190.

27. "Editorial Conference (With Wine)," *American Spectator* 1 (September 1933): 1.

28. Dreiser to Nathan, 26 May 1933, in Pizer, ed., *Theodore Dreiser: A Picture and a Criticism of Life,* 191.

29. Hapgood to "Gentlemen" (the editors of the *American Spectator*), 4 October 1933, in Elias, ed., *Letters of Theodore Dreiser,* 2: 649.

30. Hapgood, "Is Dreiser Anti-Semitic?" Further citations will appear in the text.

31. For Dreiser's similar but more explicit comment on the Nazi treatment of German Jews, see his letter to Heywood Broun, 7 January 1936, in Elias, ed., *Letters of Theodore Dreiser,* 3: 765.

32. "Dreiser Denies He Is Anti-Semitic," *New Masses* 15 (30 April 1935): 10.

33. Ibid., 10.

34. Gold, "Gun Is Loaded, Dreiser!"

35. Dreiser to Dinamov, 27 June 1935, in Elias, ed., *Letters of Theodore Dreiser,* 2: 747.

36. Dreiser to Laemmle, 23 August 1935, in Pizer, ed., *Theodore Dreiser: A Picture and a Criticism of Life,* 215–16.

37. Dreiser to Lengel, 6 May 1939, in Pizer, ed., *Theodore Dreiser: A Picture and a Criticism of Life,* 258.

38. Dreiser to Stoddart, 10 May 1939, in Pizer, ed., *Theodore Dreiser: A Picture and a Criticism of Life,* 260.

39. Dreiser to Stoddart, 22 June 1939, in Pizer, ed., *Theodore Dreiser: A Picture and a Criticism of Life,* 261.

40. Dreiser to Mencken, 3 October 1939, in Riggio, ed., *Dreiser-Mencken Letters,* 2: 651.

41. Dreiser, *"We Hold These Truths,"* 47; reprinted in Pizer, ed., *Theodore Dreiser: A Selection of Uncollected Prose,* 317–18.

42. Dreiser to Boyd, 1 May 1931, in Pizer, ed., *Theodore Dreiser: A Picture and a Criticism of Life,* 155.

43. Boyd to Dreiser, 4 May 1931, in the Beinecke Library, Yale University.

44. "Dreiser Denies He Is Anti-Semitic," *New Masses* 15 (30 April 1935): 11.

## Chapter 4: Edith Wharton and Willa Cather

1. For the editing of Wharton's letters, see Ammons, "Edith Wharton and Race," in Bell, ed., *Cambridge Companion to Edith Wharton,* 85n3; for Cather's prohibition, see Stout, *A Calendar of the Letters of Willa Cather,* xi.

2. See Birmingham, *"Our Crowd."*

3. Wharton, *Backward Glance,* 94.

4. Wharton, *The House of Mirth,* 301. Further citations will appear in the text. For further instances of Wharton's use of Darwinian imagery in the novel, see Pizer, "Naturalism of Edith Wharton's *The House of Mirth.*"

5. For discussions of the racial background of Wharton's patrician beliefs, see Ammons, "Edith Wharton and Race"; Hoeller, "'The Impossible Rosedale'"; Kassanoff, *Edith Wharton and the Politics of Race*; and Levine, *Merchant of Modernism,* 53–62.

6. See pp. 16–22 in this volume and Gossett, *Race.*

7. In addition to the essays by Ammons and Hoeller cited in notes 1 and 5 above,

the most useful of the essays concentrating on Wharton's portrayal of Rosedale are Goldman-Price, "The 'Perfect Jew' and *The House of Mirth*," in Singley, ed., *Edith Wharton's "The House of Mirth*," 163–80, and Riegel, "Rosedale and Anti-Semitism in *The House of Mirth*."

8. Ammons, "Edith Wharton and Race," 80.

9. See, in particular, Hoeller, "'The Impossible Rosedale,'" and Goldman-Price, "The 'Perfect Jew.'"

10. Randall, *Landscape and the Looking Glass,* 6–12.

11. "Old Mrs. Harris" appeared initially in the *Ladies Home Journal* (September 1932). The Wieners are also probably one of the sources for Cather's portrait in *The Song of the Lark* (1915) of the Nathanmeyers, a highly cultured Chicago Jewish family. In later years, Cather was friends with the Jewish publishers Blanche and Alfred Knopf and the Jewish musical family the Menuhins.

12. Curtin, ed., *World and the Parish,* 1: 21.

13. A number of commentators have discussed the possible impact of Isabelle McClung's marriage on Cather's depiction of Marcellus. For a reading that views the impact as significant, see Schroeter, "Willa Cather and *The Professor's House*," reprinted in Schroeter, ed., *Willa Cather and Her Critics*; for the contrary position, see Wasserman, "Cather's Semitism," in Rosowski, ed., *Cather Studies,* vol. 2.

14. Stout traces the relationship in some detail in her biography *Willa Cather: The Writer and Her World.*

15. O'Brien, "Chronology: 1916," in Cather, *Later Novels,* 951.

16. See, in addition to the sketches and stories discussed, Stout's account, in her *Willa Cather,* 152–53, of Cather's role as managing editor of *McClure's* in the magazine's 1909 publication of a series of anti-Semitic articles.

17. Cather, *Early Novels and Stories,* 94.

18. Bennett, ed., *Willa Cather's Collected Short Fiction, 1892–1912,* 47. Further citations will appear in the text.

19. Cather, *Stories, Poems, and Other Writings,* 402. Further citations will appear in the text.

20. Ibid., 459.

21. Ibid., 718.

22. For major studies of anti-Semitic strains in *The Professor's House,* see Levine, *Merchant of Modernism*; Randall, *Landscape and the Looking Glass*; Schroeter, "Willa Cather and *The Professor's House*," reprinted in Schroeter, ed., *Willa Cather and Her Critics*; and Wasserman, "Cather's Semitism," in Rosowski, ed., *Cather Studies,* vol. 2.

23. *The Professor's House,* in Cather, *Later Novels,* 233. Further citations will appear in the text.

## Epilogue

1. See in particular Martin's speech at a Socialist rally in chapter 38 of London's *Martin Eden* (1909).

# Works Cited

## Primary Works

### WILLA CATHER

"Behind the Singer Tower" (1912). In Bennett, ed., *Willa Cather's Collected Short Fiction.*

"The Diamond Mine" (1916). In O'Brien, ed., *Stories, Poems, and Other Writings.*

*Early Novels and Stories,* edited by Sharon O'Brien. New York: Library of America, 1987.

*Later Novels,* edited by Sharon O'Brien. New York: Library of America, 1990.

"The Marriage of Phaedra" (1905). In Bennett, ed., *Willa Cather's Collected Short Fiction.*

"The Old Beauty" (1948). In O'Brien, ed., *Stories, Poems, and Other Writings.*

"Old Mrs. Harris" (1932). In *Obscure Destinies.* New York: Knopf, 1932.

*The Professor's House* (1925). In O'Brien, ed., *Later Novels.*

"Scandal" (1919). In O'Brien, ed., *Stories, Poems, and Other Writings.*

*The Song of the Lark.* Boston: Houghton Mifflin, 1915.

*Stories, Poems, and Other Writings,* edited by Sharon O'Brien. New York: Library of America, 1992.

*Willa Cather's Collected Short Fiction, 1892–1912,* edited by Mildred R. Bennett. Lincoln: University of Nebraska Press, 1965.

*The World and the Parish: Willa Cather's Articles and Reviews, 1893–1902,* edited by William M. Curtin. Lincoln: University of Nebraska Press, 1970.

### THEODORE DREISER

*An American Tragedy* (1925), edited by Thomas P. Riggio. New York: The Library of America, 2003.

*The Collected Plays of Theodore Dreiser,* edited by Keith Newlin and Frederic E. Rusch.
   Albany, NY: Whitson, 2000.
*The Color of a Great City.* New York: Boni and Liveright, 1923.
*Dawn.* New York: Horace Liveright, 1931.
"Dreiser Denies He Is Anti-Semitic." *New Masses* 15 (30 April 1935): 10–11.
*Dreiser-Mencken Letters: The Correspondence of Theodore Dreiser and H. L. Mencken,
   1907–1945,* edited by Thomas P. Riggio. Philadelphia: University of Pennsylvania
   Press, 1986.
"Editorial Conference (With Wine)." *American Spectator* 1 (September 1933): 1.
*The Hand of the Potter* (1919). In Newlin and Rusch, eds., *The Collected Plays of Theo-
   dore Dreiser* (see above).
*Letters of Theodore Dreiser,* edited by Robert H. Elias. Philadelphia: University of
   Pennsylvania Press, 1959.
*Letters to Louise: Theodore Dreiser's Letters to Louise Campbell.* Philadelphia: Uni-
   versity of Pennsylvania Press, 1959.
*Theodore Dreiser: A Picture and a Criticism of Life—New Letters, Volume 1,* edited by
   Donald Pizer. Urbana: University of Illinois Press, 2008.
*Theodore Dreiser: A Selection of Uncollected Prose,* edited by Donald Pizer. Detroit:
   Wayne State University Press, 1977.
*Theodore Dreiser: Interviews,* edited by Frederic E. Rusch and Donald Pizer. Urbana:
   University of Illinois Press, 2004.
*The Titan.* New York: John Lane, 1914.
"*We Hold These Truths.*" New York: League of American Writers, 1939.

## HAMLIN GARLAND

*Afternoon Neighbors.* New York: Macmillan, 1934.
*Back-Trailers from the Middle Border.* New York: Macmillan, 1928.
*Crumbling Idols.* Chicago: Stone and Kimball, 1894.
*Hamlin Garland's Diaries,* edited by Donald Pizer. San Marino, CA: Huntington
   Library, 1968.
*My Friendly Contemporaries: A Literary Log.* New York: Macmillan, 1932.
*Roadside Meetings.* New York: Macmillan, 1930.
*Selected Letters of Hamlin Garland,* edited by Keith Newlin and Joseph B. McCullough.
   Lincoln: University of Nebraska Press, 1998.
*A Son of the Middle Border.* New York: Macmillan, 1917.
*A Spoil of Office* (1892). New York: Johnson Reprint, 1969.

## FRANK NORRIS

*The Apprenticeship Writings of Frank Norris, 1896–1898,* edited by Joseph R. McElrath,
   Jr., and Douglas K. Burgess. Philadelphia: American Philosophical Society, 1996.
"A Case for Lombroso." San Francisco *Wave* 16 (11 September 1897): 6. In McElrath
   and Burgess, eds., *Apprenticeship Writings of Frank Norris.*

"Ethics of the Freshman Rush." San Francisco *Wave* 16 (4 September 1897): 2.

*Frank Norris: Novels and Essays,* edited by Donald Pizer. New York: Library of America, 1986.

*The Literary Criticism of Frank Norris,* edited by Donald Pizer. Austin: University of Texas Press, 1964.

*McTeague* (1899), edited by Donald Pizer, 2nd ed. New York: W. W. Norton, 1997.

*Moran of the Lady Letty.* New York: Doubleday & McClure, 1898.

*The Octopus* (1901). In Pizer, ed., *Frank Norris: Novels and Essays.*

*Vandover and the Brute* (1914). In Pizer, ed., *Frank Norris: Novels and Essays.*

### EDITH WHARTON

*A Backward Glance.* New York: Appleton-Century, 1934.

*The Custom of the Country.* New York: Scribner's, 1913.

*The House of Mirth* (1905). New York: Scribner's, 1975.

"The Pot-Boiler" (1904). In *Edith Wharton, Collected Stories, 1891–1910,* edited by Maureen Howard. New York: Library of America, 2001.

## Secondary Works

Almaguer, Tomás. *Racial Fault Lines: The Historical Origins of White Supremacy in California.* Berkeley: University of California Press, 1994.

Ammons, Elizabeth. "Edith Wharton and Race." In *The Cambridge Companion to Edith Wharton,* edited by Millicent Bell, 68–86. Cambridge: Cambridge University Press, 1995.

Baldwin, Neil. *Henry Ford and the Jews: The Mass Production of Hate.* New York: Public Affairs, 2001.

Birmingham, Stephen. *"Our Crowd": The Great Jewish Families of New York.* New York: Harper & Row, 1967.

Bower, Stephanie. "Dangerous Liaisons: Prostitution, Disease, and Race in Frank Norris's Fiction." *Modern Fiction Studies* 42 (Spring 1996): 31–60.

Cahan, Abraham. "An Unusual Jewish Tragedy in an Unusual Theater." *Jewish Daily Forward,* 4 December 1921, p. 4.

Chase, Richard. *The American Novel and Its Tradition.* Garden City, NY: Doubleday, 1957.

Cohen, Naomi W. "Antisemitism in the Gilded Age: The Jewish View." *Jewish Social Studies* (Summer/Fall 1979). Reprinted in Gurock, *Anti-Semitism in America,* 263–86. New York: Routledge, 1998.

Crane, William W., and Bernard Moses. *Politics: An Introduction to the Study of Comparative Constitutional Law.* New York: Putnam's, 1886.

Dardis, Tom. *Firebrand: The Life of Horace Liveright.* New York: Random House, 1995.

Dijkstra, Bram. *Idols of Perversity: Fantasies of Feminine Evil in Fin-de-Siècle Culture.* New York: Oxford University Press, 1986.

Diggs, Annie L. "The Women in the Alliance Movement." *Arena* 6 (July 1892): 161–79.

Diner, Hasia R. *The Jews of the United States, 1654 to 2000.* Berkeley: University of California Press, 2004.

Dinnerstein, Leonard. *Antisemitism in America.* New York: Oxford University Press, 1994.

Dobkowski, Michael N. *The Tarnished Dream: The Basis of American Anti-Semitism.* Westport, CT: Greenwood, 1979.

Donnelly, Ignatius. *Caesar's Column* (1890). Cambridge, Mass.: Harvard University Press, 1960.

Ferkiss, Victor C. "Populist Influences on American Fascism." *Western Political Quarterly* (1957). Reprinted in Gurock, *Anti-Semitism in America,* 301–24. New York: Routledge, 1998.

Forrey, Robert. "The 'Jew' in Norris' *The Octopus.*" *Western States Jewish Historical Quarterly* 7 (April 1975): 201–10.

Gayley, Charles Mills. "English at the University of California." *Dial* 17 (16 July 1894): 31.

Gerber, David A., ed. *Anti-Semitism in American History.* Urbana: University of Illinois Press, 1986.

———. "Anti-Semitism and Jewish-Gentile Relations in American Historiography and the American Past." In Gerber, *Anti-Semitism in American History,* 3–54. Urbana: University of Illinois Press, 1986.

Gold, Michael. "The Gun Is Loaded, Dreiser!" *New Masses* 15 (7 May 1935): 14–15.

Goldman-Price, Irene C. "The 'Perfect Jew' and *The House of Mirth.*" In *Edith Wharton's "The House of Mirth": A Casebook,* edited by Carol J. Singley, 163–80. New York: Oxford University Press, 2003.

Gossett, Thomas F. *Race: The History of an Idea in America,* 2nd ed. New York: Oxford University Press, 1997.

Gurock, Jeffrey S., ed. *Anti-Semitism in America.* New York: Routledge, 1998.

Haller, John S. *Outcasts from Evolution: Scientific Attitudes of Racial Inferiority, 1859–1900.* Carbondale: Southern Illinois University Press, 1995.

Hapgood, Hutchins. "Is Dreiser Anti-Semitic?" *Nation* 140 (17 April 1935): 436–38.

Harap, Louis. *Creative Awakening: The Jewish Presence in Twentieth-Century American Literature, 1900–1940s.* New York: Greenwood, 1987.

———. *The Image of the Jew in American Literature,* 2nd ed. Syracuse, N.Y.: Syracuse University Press, 2003.

Harvey, William H. *Coin's Financial School* (1894), edited by Richard Hofstadter. Cambridge, Mass.: Harvard University Press, 1963.

Hicks, John D. *The Populist Revolt: A History of the Farmers' Alliance and the People's Party.* Minneapolis: University of Minnesota Press, 1931.

Higham, John. *Send These to Me: Jews and Other Immigrants in Urban America.* New York: Atheneum, 1975.

———. *Strangers in the Land: Patterns of American Nativism, 1860–1925*. New Brunswick, N.J.: Rutgers University Press, 1955.

Hoeller, Hildegard. "'The Impossible Rosedale': 'Race' and the Reading of Wharton's *The House of Mirth*." *Studies in American-Jewish Literature* 13 (1994): 14–20.

Hofstadter, Richard. *The Age of Reform: From Bryan to F. D. R.* New York: Knopf, 1955.

Horsman, Reginald. *Race and Manifest Destiny: The Origins of American Racial Anglo-Saxonism*. Cambridge, Mass.: Harvard University Press, 1981.

Jones, Howard Mumford. "The Arms of the Anglo-Saxons." In *The Theory of American Literature*. Ithaca, N.Y.: Cornell University Press, 1948.

Kahn, Sholom J. *Science and Aesthetic Judgment: A Study in Taine's Critical Method.* New York: Columbia University Press, 1953.

Kassanoff, Jennie A. *Edith Wharton and the Politics of Race*. Cambridge: Cambridge University Press, 2004.

Knight, Denise. "Charlotte Perkins Gilman and the Shadow of Racism." *American Literary Realism* 32 (Winter 2000): 159–70.

Kurtz, Benjamin P. *Charles Mills Gayley*. Berkeley: University of California Press, 1943.

Lease, Mary E. *The Problem of Civilization Solved*. Chicago: Laird and Lee, 1895.

Le Conte, Joseph. *Evolution: Its Nature, Its Evidences, and Its Relation to Religious Thought* (1888), 2nd rev. ed. New York: Appleton, 1891.

———. "The Race Problem in the South." In *Man and the State: Studies in Applied Sociology. Popular Lectures and Discussions before the Brooklyn Ethical Association.* New York: Appleton, 1892.

Lee, Albert. *Henry Ford and the Jews*. New York: Stein and Day, 1980.

Levine, Gary M. *The Merchant of Modernism: The Economic Jew in Anglo-American Literature, 1864–1939*. New York: Routledge, 2003.

Lindemann, Albert S. *Esau's Tears: Modern Anti-Semitism and the Rise of the Jews.* New York: Cambridge University Press, 1997.

Liptzin, Solomon. *The Jew in American Literature*. New York: Bloch, 1966.

Lynn, Kenneth S. *The Dream of Success: A Study of the Modern American Imagination*. Boston: Little, Brown, 1955.

Martin, Quentin E. "'This Spreading Radicalism': Hamlin Garland's *A Spoil of Office* and the Creation of True Populism." *Studies in American Fiction* 26 (1988): 29–50.

Mayo, Louise A. *The Ambivalent Image: Nineteenth-Century America's Perception of the Jew*. Rutherford, N.J.: Fairleigh Dickinson University Press, 1988.

McElrath, Joseph R., Jr. *Frank Norris and "The Wave": A Bibliography*. New York: Garland, 1988.

———, and Jesse S. Crisler. *Frank Norris: A Life*. Urbana: University of Illinois Press, 2006.

Milosz, Czeslaw, *Native Realm: A Search for Self-Definition* (1968). Berkeley: University of California Press, 1981.

Moses, Bernard. "Data of Mexican and United States History." *Papers of the California Historical Society* 1 (1887): 15–40.

Nixon, Herman C. "The Populist Movement in Iowa." *Iowa Journal of History and Politics* 24 (January 1926): 3–107.

Nordau, Max. *Degeneration.* New York: Appleton, 1895.

Nugent, Walter T. K. *The Tolerant Populists: Kansas Populism and Nativism.* Chicago: University of Chicago Press, 1963.

Pick, Daniel. *Svengali's Web: The Alien Enchanter in Modern Culture.* New Haven, Conn.: Yale University Press, 2000.

Pizer, Donald. "Dreiser and the Jews." *Dreiser Studies* 35 (Summer 2004): 3–23.

———. "Hamlin Garland in the *Standard.*" *American Literature* 26 (November 1954): 401–15.

———. *Hamlin Garland's Early Work and Career.* Berkeley: University of California Press, 1960.

———. "The Naturalism of Edith Wharton's *The House of Mirth.*" *Twentieth Century Literature* 41 (1995): 241–48.

———. *The Novels of Frank Norris.* Bloomington: University of Indiana Press, 1966.

Poliakov, Léon. *The History of Anti-Semitism,* vol. 3. New York: Vanguard, 1975.

Randall, John H. *The Landscape and the Looking Glass: Willa Cather's Search for Value.* Boston: Houghton Mifflin, 1960.

Ribuffo, Leo P. "Henry Ford and *The International Jew.*" *American Jewish History* (June 1980). In Gurock, *Anti-Semitism in America,* 413–53. New York: Routledge, 1998.

Riegel, Christian. "Rosedale and Anti-Semitism in *The House of Mirth.*" *Studies in American Fiction* 20 (Autumn 1992): 219–24.

Rockaway, Robert, and Arnon Gutfeld. "Demonic Images of the Jew in the Nineteenth-Century United States." *American Jewish History* 89 (December 2001): 355–81.

Saveth, Edward N. "Race and Nationalism in American Historiography." *Political Science Quarterly* 44 (1939): 421–41.

Schroeter, James. "Willa Cather and *The Professor's House.*" *Yale Review* 54 (Summer 1965). In *Willa Cather and Her Critics,* edited by James Schroeter, 363–81. Ithaca: Cornell University Press, 1967.

Schiff, Ellen. "Shylock's *Mishpocheh*: Anti-Semitism on the American Stage." In Gerber, *Anti-Semitism in American History,* 79–99. Urbana: University of Illinois Press, 1986.

Singerman, Robert. "The Jew as Racial Alien: The Genetic Component of American Anti-Semitism." In Gerber, *Anti-Semitism in American History,* 103–28. Urbana: University of Illinois Press, 1986.

Sorin, Gerald. *A Time for Building: The Third Migration, 1880–1920.* Baltimore: Johns Hopkins University Press, 1992.

Starr, Kevin. *Americans and the California Dream, 1850–1915.* New York: Oxford University Press, 1973.

Stout, Janis P. *A Calendar of the Letters of Willa Cather.* Lincoln: University of Nebraska Press, 2002.

———. *Willa Cather: The Writer and Her World.* Charlottesville: University Press of Virginia, 2000.

Swanberg, W. A. *Dreiser.* New York: Scribner's, 1965.

Synnott, Marcia Graham. "Anti-Semitism and American Universities: Did Quotas Follow the Jews?" In Gerber, *Anti-Semitism in American History,* 233–71. Urbana: University of Illinois Press, 1986.

Tuerk, Richard. "The *American Spectator* Symposium Controversy: Was Dreiser Anti-Semitic?" *Prospects* 16 (1991): 367–89.

Wasserman, Loretta. "Cather's Semitism." In *Cather Studies 2,* edited by Susan J. Rosowski, 1–22. Lincoln: University of Nebraska Press, 1993.

# Index

**DONALD PIZER** is Pierce Butler Professor of English emeritus at Tulane University. He has been a Guggenheim fellow and Fulbright lecturer, is the author of *The Novels of Frank Norris, The Novels of Theodore Dreiser, The Theory and Practice of American Literary Naturalism,* and other books. He is the editor of *The Cambridge Companion to American Realism and Naturalism.*

The University of Illinois Press
is a founding member of the
Association of American University Presses.

---

Composed in 10.5/13 Adobe Minion Pro
with FF Meta display
by Jim Proefrock
at the University of Illinois Press
Manufactured by Thomson-Shore, Inc.

University of Illinois Press
1325 South Oak Street
Champaign, IL 61820-6903
www.press.uillinois.edu